"Brian Zahnd's unique voice is neither 'liberal' nor 'conservative.' It is both cheekily irreverent and profoundly faithful. Above all, it is Christ-centered. He reminds me a bit of the late great William Stringfellow in his defiance of fashionable religious trends, and his fearless challenges to 'monotheistic therapeutic deism.' I just wish the church would listen to him more. Here's your chance!"

Fleming Rutledge, author of *The Crucifixion: Understanding the Death of Jesus Christ* and *Advent: The Once and Future Coming of Jesus Christ*

"In our postmodern age ablaze with skepticism and secularism, Brian Zahnd's pastoral instincts and prophetic insights encourage us not to fear the loss of all that is being burned up in the church, but to be reassured that the enduring fire of God's love is branding the entire world with the kingdom of God. This is the burning bush of a book I didn't know I needed. Turn aside, take off your shoes, and read!"

Eric E. Peterson, pastor of Colbert Presbyterian Church and author of *Letters to a Young Congregation*

"What we need is a wise, unflustered, generous, and disruptive friend. Brian Zahnd is this kind of friend. Engaging wounds inflicted by the church, questions haunting the mind, and those aches deep in the soul, Brian writes as one who has truly encountered Jesus, even while wrestling in the dark. Brian writes with the curiosity and daring of one who has learned to trust the long lyric of love."

Winn Collier, director of the Eugene Peterson Center for Christian Imagination at Western Theological Seminary and author of *Love Big, Be Well: Letters to a Small-Town Church*

"Though this beautiful, compassionate, and intelligently crafted book is for everyone, it is especially for those who feel their faith is barely hanging by fingerholds over the abyss of unbelief. Before you let go, take a moment and a breath, and read this book. You are not alone. You do matter."

Wm. Paul Young, author of *The Shack*

"Brian's words are a pleasing aroma, pastoral and full of love, reminding me—in the midst of what has often been my own terrifying disillusionment—that Jesus Christ remains the participatory God who empathizes with my lostness but does not leave me there, alone. How I have longed for faith informed by the kind of love that casts out fear, but what a frightening thing it is—to lose the fear that has for so long equated itself with faith! *When Everything's on Fire*, indeed."

Levi Macallister, "Levi the Poet"

"Is it possible to hold on to Christian faith in an age of unbelief? This is one of the many questions Brian Zahnd wisely and prophetically engages in *When Everything's on Fire*. It's a massive question that requires a level of exploration many are not adept to speak on. But Brian has time and time again demonstrated an uncanny ability to help us navigate this present age. Whether you are losing faith or want to help others hold on to it, we would do well to have Zahnd take our hand and be our guide."

Rich Villodas, lead pastor of New Life Fellowship and author of *The Deeply Formed Life*

"If your faith is thin, if you've placed trust in what has proven to be untrustworthy, if you're wondering if it's still possible to be a Christian in the current fiery melee of the world, the church, and your own head and heart, come stand with Brian. If you stand there long enough, you will find yourself enfolded by Jesus' first and last word over you, which is not righteous certitude, paper-thin apologetic, or religious sentiment but blazing, resurrected love."

Cherith Fee Nordling, sessional professor of theology, Regent College

"I believe the book you are holding now is one that truly only Brian Zahnd could write, and the precise book we needed him to write in this particular moment. His gift is clarity, and the way he focuses his prophetic vision here is so lucid, singular, and laser focused, it is almost blinding. Zahnd does not offer us certainty in uncertain times, which is always just a bad magic trick, anyway—he offers something much better: beauty. This is a flaming, scorchingly beautiful vision of faith in a world where faith has left many of us in the cold. Prepare to be burned."

Jonathan Martin, author of *The Road Away from God* and *How to Survive a Shipwreck*

"There is no better guide than Brian Zahnd for someone who is in a season of life when everything's on fire. Brian's ability to speak as both prophet and pastor illuminates a path forward for those who face a dark night of unknowing. Rather than offering pseudocertainty and pithy apologetical arguments—rooted as they often are in modernity's gods—Brian invites readers to embrace the greatest mystery of all: a God who *actually looks like Jesus*! From now on, when I have a friend and/or member of my congregation who is going through a faith crisis, *When Everything's on Fire* will be the first book I hand them."

Kurt Willems, pastor, author of *Echoing Hope: How the Humanity of Jesus Redeems Our Pain*

WHEN

EVERYTHING'S ON FIRE

FAITH FORGED
FROM THE ASHES

BRIAN ZAHND

An imprint of InterVarsity Press
Downers Grove, Illinois

InterVarsity Press
P.O. Box 1400, Downers Grove, IL 60515-1426
ivpress.com
email@ivpress.com

InterVarsity Press® is the book-publishing division of InterVarsity Christian Fellowship/USA®, a movement of students and faculty active on campus at hundreds of universities, colleges, and schools of nursing in the United States of America, and a member movement of the International Fellowship of Evangelical Students. For information about local and regional activities, visit intervarsity.org.

While any stories in this book are true, some names and identifying information may have been changed to protect the privacy of individuals.

Published in association with The Bindery Agency, www.TheBinderyAgency.com.

Cover design and image composite: David Fassett
Interior design: Jeanna Wiggins
Images: leaf vines: © Nature Desaign / iStock / Getty Images Plus
*   black ink rolled on to white paper: ©IntergalacticDesignStudio / E+ / Getty Images*
*   rolled black ink on white paper: ©IntergalacticDesignStudio / E+ / Getty Images*

ISBN 978-1-5140-0333-6 (print)
ISBN 978-1-5140-0334-3 (digital)

Printed in the United States of America ⊗

Library of Congress Cataloging-in-Publication Data
Names: Zahnd, Brian, author.
Title: When everything's on fire : faith forged from the ashes / Brian Zahnd.
Description: Downers Grove, IL : InterVarsity Press, [2021] | Includes bibliographical references.
Identifiers: LCCN 2021030769 (print) | LCCN 2021030770 (ebook) | ISBN 9781514003336 (hardcover) | ISBN 9781514003343 (ebook)
Subjects: LCSH: Faith. | Christianity—21st century. | Christianity and culture. | Postmodernism—Religious aspects—Christianity. | Apologetics.
Classification: LCC BV4637 .Z34 2021 (print) | LCC BV4637 (ebook) | DDC 234/.23—dc23
LC record available at https://lccn.loc.gov/2021030769
LC ebook record available at https://lccn.loc.gov/2021030770

| P | 25 | 24 | 23 | 22 | 21 | 20 | 19 | 18 | 17 | 16 | 15 | 14 | 13 | 12 | 11 | 10 | 9 | 8 | 7 | 6 | 5 | 4 | 3 | 2 | 1 |
| Y | 38 | 37 | 36 | 35 | 34 | 33 | 32 | 31 | 30 | 29 | 28 | 27 | 26 | 25 | 24 | 23 | 22 | 21 |

For Anthony and António

How do you know but ev'ry Bird that cuts the airy way,
Is an immense world of delight, clos'd by your senses five?

WILLIAM BLAKE

CONTENTS

FOREWORD
Bradley Jersak

Frankenstein and Faust are yet the rage
Unspeakable, the severing damage done
Yet on the wind, the distant sound of drum
And the sweetness of the sage
Still might come a kinder age.

STEVE BELL, *WOULDN'T YOU LOVE TO KNOW*

F riends of the truth, the book you are about to read brought me tears of both grief and joy. I moaned over the darkness revealed as darkness, and laughed with hope as Easter dawn was unveiled afresh. This book is the word of the Lord (thanks be to God). I know this because "the testimony of Jesus is the spirit of prophecy," and that Spirit reverberates throughout these pages.

Brian Zahnd is a unique blend of pastor, prophet, and poet—
he's a preacher, a philosopher, and a mystic. He's a man of prayer
who teaches us to pray. No, he's not Jesus—but he does know him.
They sit together daily. From his friendship with Jesus Christ, BZ's
words and works emerge as a blazing minority report, a synthesis
of beauty, truth, and justice mediated by cruciform love. How
grateful I am for his witness! How happy I am that our lives have
become a collaboration.

I was so gratified to see Brian's deep engagement with Nietzsche,
Dostoevsky, Kierkegaard, et al., given our mutual regard for their
important contributions and critiques of this present darkness. But
most of all, I am thrilled (but unsurprised) to see how he walks the
confused, the disillusioned, and the deluded into the light. In that
sense, Brian strikes me as a sort of Socrates fulfilled in Christ. Let
me explain . . . no, there is too much. Let me sum up.

In Plato's *Republic*, the sage Socrates offers his famous but oft
misunderstood cave analogy. In the bowels of a dark cave, we find a
company of dreary figures bound in chains, so immobile that they
can only stare straight ahead. They peer at the cave wall, fixated on
shadows projected by objects passing in front of a fire behind them.
They can imagine no other reality than those dancing shadows. Their
myopia anticipates the twenty-first-century masses, mesmerized by
our smartphones, deluded by the strange notion that whatever their
blue light glow says is real. Our culture's addiction to entertainment
"news," conspiracy theories, and the matrix of spectrum ideology is
a photoshopped pseudo-reality with bad lip-syncing.

Inexplicably, which is to say *by grace*, one day, one of the prisoner's
chains are broken. Socrates doesn't say how. But the psalmist does:

Some sat in darkness and in gloom,
    prisoners in misery and in irons,
for they had rebelled against the words of God,
    and spurned the counsel of the Most High.

Their hearts were bowed down with hard labor;
  they fell down, with no one to help.
Then they cried to the LORD in their trouble,
  and he saved them from their distress;
he brought them out of darkness and gloom,
  and broke their bonds asunder. (Ps 107:10-14)

Now back to *The Republic*. Initially, the prisoner who turns around sees a campfire. Some honest-to-goodness light at last! Manmade light, to be sure, but it's a start. Campfires are nice. They're warm in a comforting way. I can watch the flames for hours. Hypnotized. And never leave the cave.

All of you are kindlers of fire,
  lighters of firebrands.
Walk in the flame of your fire,
  and among the brands that you have kindled!
This is what you shall have from my hand:
  you shall lie down in torment. (Is 50:11)

Isaiah saw the peril three centuries before Plato. What peril? The second delusion: that all those aha moments of wokeness we experience in personal therapy or social movements (however good) add up to enlightenment. As if my deconstruction and newfound self-awareness are ultimate reality. Not so much. Campfires are a good waypoint on our journey up and out, but attachment to them means we're still stuck in the cave.

This is where Plato's Socrates gets misunderstood. The cave, for him, is not our earthly existence. He's not a Gnostic trying to escape the material world any more than Paul was. The cave for him is "the world" of 1 John 2:15-17—the worldly systems defined by "the lust of the flesh, the lust of the eyes, and the pride of life" (NIV). That world and its desires, says John, are passing away. A darkness that in light of the Christ is already fading.

At this point, someone needs to drag the prisoner from the cave. Who does this? Maybe Socrates thought it was a mentor like himself or his dialogical teaching. Maybe that's BZ's role. What does resonate with me is the *dragging*. What drags me out of my slumber is often the cold slap of tragedy or the pain of my own self-harm or the rude shock of discovering I've believed lies for my whole life.

In any case, that gets us to the threshold of the cave—our first glimpse of the true light of the sun. For Plato, the sun represents God or the Good. Beholding the sun is quite a shock at first. Your eyes have to adjust. Maybe you have to start by squinting at reflections of the sun in a lake. Might I suggest the Sea of Galilee? But the point is that the same sun that created your eyes now also illuminates them and everything around you. You're not leaving this existence, but you're seeing that it's bigger and brighter and more ablaze with glory than you'd ever imagined. The whole world becomes Moses' transfigured shrub.

The Christian mystical tradition calls this stage of growth and revelation "illumination" because, at last, you're beholding the source of the light and truth itself. And who is this light but the sun of righteousness (Mal 4:2) who came into the world, the true light from light who shines on all humanity (Jn 1:9)?

Socrates, however, does not stop at illumination. The prisoner who has been released from his chains, dragged from the cave, and has seen the light doesn't rest self-satisfied in an arrivals lounge. The light also fills those who've seen it with compassion for those still bound in darkness. They feel the call to reenter the cave with the good news. For Socrates, this represents the philosopher who has found enlightenment and is now compelled to reenter the mess of city politics to advocate for a just society. He warns that returning to the darkness from the safety of one's contemplative island can be disorienting and dangerous. Having seen the light, those who revisit the cave are again disoriented. It's hard to see in the dark. To the prisoners there, you just look like a staggering drunk, tripping your way to the restroom. In fact, he says, if they could, they'd attack you. Brian knows this.

Elsewhere in *The Republic*, we see a demythologized version of the story. We read a prophecy, many centuries before Christ, where Glaucon (Plato's older brother) warns that if the Good were to manifest in this world, it would come as the perfectly righteous man. And how would he be received? We would inevitably arrest him, beat him, and *crucify* him. Yes, he uses that word.

And in this sense, Socrates is fulfilled in Christ, for Christ *did* enter this world that was shrouded by darkness, and he was murdered on a cross. But what Socrates did not foresee was that the darkness could not overcome the just Man and by his resurrection, Christ "destroy[ed] the death shroud that enfolds all peoples" (Is 25:7 NIV). As we Orthodox sing repeatedly during the Pascha celebration,

> Christ is risen from the dead,
> trampling down death by death
> and upon those in the tomb, bestowing life.

I say all that to introduce you again to a Jesus-loving Socratic sage and light-bearer. May God use his beautiful gospel to break chains, bring clarity, and lead us up and out into the light, where we behold with unveiled faces the glory of God in the face of Jesus Christ.

Fiat Lux

PRELUDE

I n fall 2019, my wife and I made our third pilgrimage on the Camino de Santiago. Walking the Camino has become one of the great passions of my life. The pilgrim life suits me—at least for a few weeks every few years. We take our first step on the Camino in the French village of Saint-Jean-Pied-de-Port in the Pyrenees Mountains, and then forty days and five hundred miles later, we arrive at the cathedral in Santiago de Compostela, Spain.

But the old adage "it's the journey, not the destination that matters most" is particularly true of modern pilgrimage. If the destination is the point, I can get to Santiago from anywhere in the world in a matter of hours. But that's not the point. The point is the long walk itself and the simplified life of being a pilgrim—it's a respite "far from the madding crowd" of modernity. For forty days and forty nights, our lives are reduced to the blessed singularity of walking from town to town, from church to church, from one lodging to the next, each day moving a bit closer to Santiago. We don't dart here and there, back and forth in a frenzy; we don't speed through the world in mechanized transport; we just journey steadily westward, never moving any faster than footspeed. The slowness is the point. Because when we slow down enough over a protracted period, we settle into a more contemplative state. The true destination of my pilgrim journey isn't Santiago but the stillness of soul conducive to contemplation.

To walk the Camino de Santiago is a deeply spiritual experience. Every pilgrim, no matter how secular in their philosophy, senses this and it's a frequent topic of conversation. "The Camino will provide" is a common expression among pilgrims. It means that no matter what you need, it will somehow turn up as you walk the Way. I've found that this is true on many levels. The spirituality of the Camino is a precious anomaly in our disenchanted age. The Camino is also religious—by which I mean you will pass countless churches, chapels, and crucifixes. Virtually every pilgrim will attend at least one Mass to receive a pilgrim blessing. You will almost certainly find lodging several nights in a monastery. It's impossible not to sense the religious devotion of the millions of medieval pilgrims who walked the road to Santiago in their pre-modern world.

It's considered incontrovertible that Europe is thoroughly secular while America clings to Christianity. But that has not been my experience. When I'm in Europe, I sense deep, though often buried and forgotten, Christian roots; while in America, I encounter a thin veneer of civil religion disguising a deeply secular core. Contrary to what some may think, the soil of Americanized Christianity is not well-suited to nourishing or sustaining Christian faith. This is what I was thinking about as I walked the Camino in fall 2019.

I was keenly aware of the faith-challenging fiery ordeal that Western Christians are currently passing through, and I began to formulate some ideas of what I would like to say to those whose faith is in the crucible. Two weeks and two hundred miles into the Camino, I sat for several hours on a terrace in Castrojeriz—a lovely hilltop village that has welcomed pilgrims for over seven hundred years—and outlined the eleven chapters of this book, giving it the title *When Everything's on Fire.* I began the writing process in January. At the beginning of 2020, it seemed like everything was on fire, and then—*everything was on fire!* A global pandemic. An economic crisis. A day of reckoning for America's systemic racial injustice. Nationwide protests. More police shootings of unarmed Black men. More unrest. More scandals in the church. More politicization of the Christian faith. More political vitriol and violence. More enflamed division. More people losing faith. Indeed, everything's on fire!

But all is not lost—far from it. Even when everything seems to be on fire, faith is still possible. Faith does not have to perish in the ashes of a theological deconstruction. The particular challenges of our secular age do not have to be a dead end for faith. There is a way forward. The apostle Peter speaks of a faith that is more precious than gold because it has been refined by fire (1 Pet 1:7). It *is* possible to forge a valid and vibrant faith from the ashes of fiery testing. That's what I want to discuss. I wish that you and I could walk together for few days on the Camino de Santiago and have many long conversations about the possibility of Christian faith in an epoch of unbelief. And who knows, maybe that will happen someday. But for now, this book will have to suffice. As you read, try to think of me as a fellow pilgrim on the journey of life who, for a little while, seeks to be your walking companion and conversation partner.

Allons! Whoever you are come travel with me!
Traveling with me you find what never tires.
The earth never tires,
The earth is rude, silent, incomprehensible at first,
Nature is rude and incomprehensible at first,
Be not discouraged, keep on, there are divine things well envelop'd,
I swear to you there are divine things more
beautiful than words can tell.

WALT WHITMAN, "SONG OF THE OPEN ROAD"

PART 1

WHEN EVERYTHING'S ON FIRE

1

THE MADMAN'S LANTERN

O nce upon a time, we all believed in God. In an earlier epoch, we believed in God (or gods) as effortlessly as we believed in the firm ground beneath our feet and the expanse of sky above our heads. An ancient Greek poet expressed it like this in a hymn to Zeus (later reappropriated by the apostle Paul): "In him we live and move and have our being" (Acts 17:28). For the ancients, the divine was as immanent as the air they breathed. But that was before everything was on fire. That was before the conflagration of world wars, before the skies over Auschwitz were darkened with human ash, before the ominous mushroom clouds over Hiroshima and Nagasaki, before the world witnessed twin pillars of smoke rising into the September sky over Manhattan, before long-venerated institutions were engulfed in the flames of scandal, before the scorched-earth assault on Christianity by its cultured despisers. Today, it's harder to believe, harder to hold on to faith, and nearly impossible to embrace religion with unjaded innocence. We live in a time when everything is on fire and the faith of millions is imperiled.

So, is Christian faith still viable in an age of unbelief?

Yes, it is possible. I can bear witness. My own faith has passed through the flames of modernity and is alive and well. I've faced the most potent challenges to Christian faith head-on and lived to tell the tale as a believing Christian. A healthy, flourishing faith is possible in the twenty-first century, but we need to acknowledge that we are passing through a time of rising skepticism, cynicism, and secularism. Our age is no friend to faith, and the challenges we face are real. I hear the melancholy whispers of Galadriel at the beginning of *The Lord of the Rings*: "The world is changed: I feel it in the water, I feel it in the earth, I smell it in the air. Much that once was is lost, for none now live who remember it."[1]

"Much that once was is lost"—many of us resonate with that sentiment. The loss has been sudden and precipitous. The Western world entered the twentieth century still tethered to a much older world—a world where people felt the immanence of God. But somewhere along the way through that tumultuous century, the cord was severed and we entered a new world—a world where God seems to have gone missing. The ethos of our age might be described as the felt absence of God. Something has been lost and in the Western world, Christianity is in decline. Most denominations are losing membership and the fastest-growing religious category in America is "none." For believers who, in their anxiety and frustration, recklessly frame this phenomenon in culture-war terms, this has produced considerable consternation. But their culture-war-induced rage only adds fuel to the fire of post-Christian attitudes. Being angry with modern people for losing their faith is like being angry with medieval people for dying of the plague. Something has happened in our time. Just as something happened in the Middle Ages that imperiled the lives of medieval people, something has happened in late modernity that has imperiled the faith of modern people. Something has crippled shared religious belief in the Western world over the past century. And no one foresaw it more clearly than Friedrich Nietzsche, the famed German philosopher and vehement critic of Christianity.

In 1882—seven years before his descent into madness— Friedrich Nietzsche published a parable called *The Madman*. In the parable, a madman comes into a village on a bright, sunny morning holding aloft a lantern and crying, "I seek God! I seek God!" This absurdity elicits laughter and mockery from the villagers. The madman then jumps into their midst with a wild look in his eyes,

> "Whither is God?" he cried; "I will tell you. *We have killed him*—you and I. All of us are his murderers. But how did we do this? How could we drink up the sea? Who gave us the sponge to wipe away the entire horizon? What were we doing when we unchained this earth from its sun? Whither is it moving now? Whither are we moving? Away from all suns? Are we not plunging continually? Backward, sideward, forward, in all directions? Is there still any up or down? Are we not straying, as through an infinite nothing? Do we not feel the breath of empty space? Has it not become colder? Is not night continually closing in on us? Do we not need to light lanterns in the morning? Do we hear nothing as yet of the noise of the gravediggers who are burying God? Do we smell nothing as yet of the divine decomposition? Gods, too, decompose. God is dead. God remains dead. And we have killed him."[2]

After his rant, the madman smashes the lantern on the ground before his astonished listeners and says, "I have come too early, my time is not yet. This tremendous event is still on its way."[3] The parable ends with the madman going into churches and singing a requiem for God.

It's a remarkably powerful and clairvoyant piece of imaginative writing that foresaw the decline of Christian faith in the twentieth century. Nietzsche's madman smashing the lantern might be seen as something like Mrs. O'Leary's cow kicking over the lantern in the barn. O'Leary's cow set Chicago on fire, and Nietzsche's madman set the Western world on fire. I don't mean Nietzsche *caused* what is happening to Christian faith in Western Europe and North America, but he foresaw it with such clarity that it's as if he were present for the first flickering of what has become a raging inferno. In 1882, Nietzsche proclaimed that "God is dead," though at that time the vast majority of people in Europe called themselves Christian and attended church. But by 1966, things had changed. That year, *Time* magazine put this controversial question on what is probably its most famous cover: *Is God Dead?* What seemed like the ravings of a madman in the 1880s became a legitimate question in the 1960s. In Nietzsche's parable, when the madman saw that the villagers were not prepared to hear his prophecy, he simply said, "I have come too early, my time is not yet." But his time has now come. Is God dead? Today, it's an even more relevant question than when it first appeared on the cover of *Time*.

LUNCH WITH NIETZSCHE

I have a fantasy of having lunch with Nietzsche at some cozy café in Basel, Switzerland. If my fantasy were to come true, I would have to spend the first fifteen minutes catching him up with what has happened over the past century or so—from the rise of mechanized warfare in the First World War to the rise of weaponized disinformation in the digital age and the steady rise of atheism all along the way. I don't think Nietzsche would be surprised. He saw most of it coming. I've read much of Nietzsche's work and have to admit I have a fondness for this troubled and provocative philosopher. He was a towering intellect, a tremendous writer, a savage polemicist, and the most formidable critic of Christianity in the modern era. And if one is offended by his hostile disposition toward Christianity, it should be remembered that his caustic assaults were more of an attack on moribund Christendom as a cultural artifact than on a faith centered on the life and teachings of Jesus. Indeed, Nietzsche at times seems to have a begrudging admiration for Jesus of Nazareth.

I readily admit to agreeing with a good deal of what Nietzsche writes. His critique of nineteenth-century European Christianity is often as accurate as it is scathing. Even if in the end, Nietzsche is tragically wrong about many important things, I still respect his analysis of the problem. So what does Nietzsche mean by what is probably his most famous aphorism: *God is dead*? In *The Gay Science* (or *The Joyful Wisdom*)—the book that contains the parable of the madman—Nietzsche says, "The greatest recent event—that 'God is dead,' that the belief in the Christian god has become unbelievable—is already beginning to cast its first shadows over Europe."[4]

Even though it's now associated with him, Nietzsche didn't coin the phrase *God is dead*. As the son of a Lutheran pastor, he would have heard that line in a Lutheran Holy Saturday hymn. And although Nietzsche had become an atheist, in his aphorism "God is dead," he doesn't simply mean that God doesn't exist. Rather, he means that he foresees how belief in God will soon cease to be the organizing principle of European civilization. Nietzsche perceived that the Christian bourgeoisie already lived as if God did not exist, even if their religious philosophy had not caught up with their actual practice. PKs (pastors' kids) like Nietzsche are often keenly aware of the hypocrisy of parishioners. Nietzsche understood that people often live as practical atheists before they come out of the closet as professed atheists. In the 1880s, Nietzsche was saying that Western civilization had already in practice become atheistic, even if most people didn't know it yet. With the prescience of a prophet—albeit a mad prophet—Nietzsche anticipates the rise of a secular age where faith is increasingly pushed to the periphery. And he was entirely correct in his prophecy.

Yet unlike the smug new atheists, Nietzsche did not gloat over the demise of Christianity. Rather, he feared that it would leave nothing but the void of nihilism that he described as "an infinite nothing." He spoke of the loss of Christian faith as a sponging away of the horizon, meaning that Western culture would suffer a crisis of moral vertigo, unable to define what constitutes the Good. Nietzsche knew that if culture becomes atheistic without supplying a new organizing center to replace what was once occupied by God, that culture is doomed to drift into cold and empty nihilism. He describes it as the earth being unchained from the sun. Unlike the zealous new atheists, Nietzsche didn't say "Hooray! We've got rid of God! Now everything will get better!" Nietzsche was much more sober and feared that life in a world that had abandoned God would become petty and pointless.

Nevertheless, Nietzsche was ready for the world to take the bold step and move on without God. Nietzsche was a kind of John the Baptist preparing the way for a new secular age. Nietzsche *hoped* that this new age would see the rise of the *Übermensch*, the overman, the superman; he *hoped* that through what he called the will to power heroic men (and yes, it would be men) would lead humanity into a new dawn of greatness—a theme the Nazis would exploit to horrific ends.[5] Nietzsche *hoped* that men as gallant gods would rise to occupy the place previously occupied by the Judeo-Christian God. But he also *feared* that instead of the superman, the future would belong to what he called "the last man." In *Thus Spoke Zarathustra*, he writes,

> Behold! I show you *the last man*.
> "What is love? What is creation? What is longing? What is a star"—so asks the last man and he blinks.
> The earth has become small, and on it hops the last man who makes everything small. His species is ineradicable like that of the flea; the last man lives longest.
> "We have invented happiness"—say the last men, and blink.[6]

For Nietzsche, the last man (his metaphor for the final development of a failed humanity) is an incurious utilitarian who can only see value in terms of commerce. The last man has no grander ambition than a kind of sedated happiness, and Nietzsche thought that making happiness our prime objective was an unworthy goal for human life. The *Übermensch* wants much more out of life than mere happiness. For the *Übermensch*, the struggle itself brings more meaning to life than personal contentment. From Nietzsche, we get the famous saying "What doesn't kill me makes me stronger."[7] Nietzsche, who was a mountaineer himself, would have appreciated George Mallory's famous answer to the question of why he was climbing Mount Everest: "Because it's there."

But the last man can never understand the value of a noble struggle. For the last man, climbing a mountain or exploring the ocean or creating art or gaining an education can only be worth the effort if it serves a utilitarian end. The last man has no interest in adventure, exploration, art, or education *for its own sake*. The last man will climb a mountain only if he has a corporate sponsor; he'll explore the ocean only if he can drill for oil; he'll create art only if it will sell; he'll get an education only if it will land him a high-paying job. The last man just wants a comfortable life and some prosaic happiness. I imagine Nietzsche's last man sitting in a recliner, remote in hand, surfing seven hundred channels, muttering, "We have invented happiness," and then blinking stupidly. If Nietzsche's *Übermensch* was a kind of heroic Greek god, his last man is basically an incurious couch potato. That it would not be the Greek gods but the apathetic, entertainment-addled last man who would follow the death of God was Nietzsche's biggest fear.

Nietzsche was a serious thinker and his arguments need to be taken seriously, and I've tried to do so. It's why I've read so much of his work. He was brilliant and perceptive, but in the end, he was wrong. I believe history bears this out. I suppose if I did get to have my fantasy lunch with Nietzsche, I'd have to tell him the bad news that his dreamed-of *Übermensch* turned out to be a monster and that his dreaded last man seems to be the inevitable end of his philosophical trajectory. It would probably be an awkward lunch. Maybe I don't want to have that lunch with Nietzsche after all—it would be just too sad.

As I said, I have a fondness for him. I wouldn't relish telling Nietzsche that his philosophy doesn't lead to a new heroic age but only to the dead end of nihilism—the very thing he feared. I find it easy to forgive Nietzsche's vicious attacks on religion because his criticism of the cultural Christianity he saw in late-nineteenth-century Europe was essentially the same criticism leveled by the Danish philosopher and Christian thinker Søren Kierkegaard. The difference between these two existential philosophers is that while Kierkegaard believed that within the dry husk of Christendom there was the living seed of the Word of God, Nietzsche believed that Christianity was nothing but an empty shell. To put it very simply, in his criticism of Christianity, Kierkegaard still believed in Christ while Nietzsche did not. In the end, Kierkegaard took the better road.

THE MASTERS OF SUSPICION

Nietzsche belongs to a trinity of nineteenth-century thinkers that Paul Ricoeur called the "masters of suspicion." These masters of suspicion—Friedrich Nietzsche, Karl Marx, and Sigmund Freud— were all suspicious of the same thing: the possibility of altruistic love as a primary motive. For Nietzsche, Marx, and Freud, the claim that at the heart of Christian faith is found pure love is met with resolute skepticism—they simply don't believe that people can be truly motivated by love of God and love of neighbor. Marx says our motives are mostly about money; Freud says our motives are mostly about sex; Nietzsche says our motives are mostly about power. Nietzsche in particular insisted that Christian love was nothing but what he called "slave morality"—a way for the weak to manipulate the strong, a way for the slave to covertly express his *ressentiment* toward his master.

According to Nietzsche, the slave morality of Christian love prevented humanity from rising to its potential greatness. Nietzsche thought that the ideal of Christian love kept humanity weak, ignoble, and sick. He was convinced that it was time for humanity to cast off the pretense of altruistic love and, through a fierce will to power, become supermen who march into a new heroic age unshackled from the ball and chain of Christian slave morality. This is certainly how the Nazis read Nietzsche as they venerated *Beyond Good and Evil, The Twilight of the Idols, The Antichrist,* and other Nietzschean works as their canonical texts. The Nazis were consciously attempting to live out Nietzsche's philosophy; they were deliberately trying to be the supermen that Nietzsche imagined. Nietzsche was certainly not a genocidal anti-Semite, but powerful ideas can have consequences—and Nietzsche knew this. In *Ecce Homo,* he writes,

I know my fate. One day there will be associated with my name the recollection of something frightful—a crisis like no other before on earth, of the profoundest collision of conscience, a decision evoked against everything that until then had been believed in, demanded, sanctified. I am not a man, I am dynamite.[8]

Unfortunately, these words turned out more horrifyingly true than Nietzsche could have imagined in 1889. Of course, Nietzsche did not foresee or intend the Holocaust, but when you play with fire, sometimes it gets out of control and burns everything to the ground. And lest you think I'm being unfair to Nietzsche by connecting him to Hitler and Nazism, allow me to cite French philosopher and founder of deconstruction theory, Jacques Derrida: "The future of the Nietzschean text is not closed. But if within the still-open contours of an era, the only politics calling itself—proclaiming itself—Nietzschean will have been a Nazi one, then this is necessarily significant and must be questioned in all of its consequences."[9]

Nietzsche was accurate in his prediction that Western civilization was entering an epoch where God would no longer be the assumed center of society, but he was horribly wrong in thinking that the way forward lay with the *Übermensch*. For all of his brilliance, Nietzsche was tragically naive in thinking that his imagined superman with his dark fascination with shaping the world through a violent will to power would lead anywhere other than to death camps and a continent in ruin. Nietzsche was right in his diagnosis of the problem but criminally wrong in his solution.

A CHRISTIAN CRITIQUE OF CHRISTENDOM

Where does this leave us now? The lantern has been smashed, the brazen assertion that God is dead is ringing in our ears, and everything seems to be on fire. What shall we do? Is it inevitable that we follow a path foretold by Nietzsche that leads to the end of Christian faith, or is there a way to take seriously what Nietzsche heralds and still believe? Nietzsche saw something real looming on the horizon of the twentieth century, but is the madman right when he says, "What after all are these churches now if they are not the tombs and sepulchers of God?"[10] Is that true, or does the church still have a future as a living witness to a risen Christ?

In recent years, we've seen believers, pastors, and well-known Christian leaders publicly lose their faith. This phenomenon is happening with increasing regularity. Does that mean we who still believe are simply whistling past the graveyard and stubbornly forestalling our own inevitable loss of faith? Here is the big question: *Is it possible to hold on to Christian faith in an age of unbelief?* The answer is *yes!* Certainly, contemporary Nietzsches are announcing the impossibility of Christian faith, but there are also trustworthy guides who can say with Fyodor Dostoevsky, "I believe in Christ and confess him not like some child; my hosanna has passed through an enormous furnace of doubt."[11]

It's helpful to keep in mind that what Nietzsche critiqued about Christianity, Kierkegaard also equally critiqued—and he could be every bit as polemical as Nietzsche. In 1855, Kierkegaard published *Attack Upon "Christendom."* Kierkegaard believed that the nominal state-sponsored Lutheranism of Denmark was quite nearly the very opposite of the demanding Christianity set forth in the New Testament, and he attacked it head-on. Here's an example of the kind of polemic found in Kierkegaard's *Attack*:

> I might be tempted to make to Christendom a proposal different from that of the Bible Society. Let us collect all the New Testaments we have, let us bring them out to an open square or up to some summit of a mountain, and while we all kneel let one man speak to God thus: "Take this book back again; we men, such as we are now, are not fit to go in for this sort of thing, it only makes us unhappy." This is my proposal, that like those inhabitants in Gerasa we beseech Christ to depart

from our borders. This would be an honest and human way of talking—rather different from the disgusting hypocritical priestly fudge about life having no value for us without the priceless blessing which is Christianity.[12]

Kierkegaard continues in this vein of biting satire for three hundred blistering pages. He may have even outdone Nietzsche in his withering assault on the languid and self-satisfied state-sponsored Christianity of his day. Though Kierkegaard never read Nietzsche (Kierkegaard died before Nietzsche began his career), he is attacking Nietzsche's last man pretending to be a Christian. Kierkegaard could have written, "The last man says, 'I'm saved,' and blinks." Both of these powerful thinkers despised the easy seduction of lazy groupthink—Kierkegaard called it "the crowd" and Nietzsche called it "the herd," but they both said the same thing. Nietzsche's last man follows the herd and Kierkegaard's Christendom follows the crowd. Both philosophers urge their readers to take responsibility for their lives and act with conviction and courage. But for all their similarities—and they are remarkably alike!—they ultimately reached very different conclusions. Kierkegaard held a deep and abiding faith in Jesus Christ. It's fair to say that his Christian faith informed *all* of his philosophical work. Kierkegaard was able to make the vital distinction between a failed Christendom and a triumphant Christ.

One of the great tragedies in the history of philosophy is that Nietzsche never read Kierkegaard. (Kierkegaard was virtually unknown outside of Copenhagen before Nietzsche's mental collapse in 1890.) I suppose my real fantasy is that Kierkegaard could have lunch with Nietzsche. I think they would have thoroughly understood one another and probably enjoyed one another's company. I can imagine Kierkegaard listening to Nietzsche, nodding his head and saying, "Yes, yes, yes! But have you thought about *this*?" What a fascinating conversation that would be! Nietzsche in conversation with Kierkegaard; skepticism in conversation with faith; "I've lost my faith" in conversation with "I still believe." That's what I hope this book can be. I hope it can be my, "Yes, yes, yes! But have you thought about this?" conversation with those who feel like their faith is hanging by a thread. This is my long lunch conversation with those who still hold out hope for an authentic faith but are asking, "What can we do when everything is on fire?"

DECONSTRUCTING DECONSTRUCTION

2

I n recent years, there's been much talk in Christian circles about *deconstruction*. The term is used to describe a crisis of Christian faith that leads to either a reevaluation of Christianity or sometimes a total abandonment of Christianity. Not long ago, I had dinner with a young and recently former pastor who told me he had begun listening to a popular post-Christian podcast and, within six months, had become an atheist. He described this sudden loss of faith as his "deconstruction." In his case, deconstruction was more of a demolition from which nothing survived. I found his story of a faith shipwrecked on the rocks of a podcast both rash and sad. Of course, I've heard these stories before—they've become the tale du jour in certain circles. The stories of Christian leaders announcing their agnosticism are becoming disconcertingly commonplace.

But there's always more to the story than "young pastor meets skepticism-inducing podcast." Drastic deconstructions like this are often a reaction to some kind of fundamentalism. A faith

formed in rigid, defensive fundamentalism stands on far more precarious ground than is supposed by its adherents. In fact, in a
secular age, faith founded on fundamentalist certitude is increasingly untenable. For example, when a Christian formed in fundamentalism reads Genesis as an empirical account of the age of the
universe and the origin of the species instead of an inspired poetic
revelation showing that all of creation comes from the sheer gra-
tuity of a benevolent God and that creation is itself inherently good,
they're just one PBS science documentary away from a deconstruction so severe that nothing remains of their Christian faith.

An empiricist reading of mythic literature is entirely wrong-
headed. The deep wisdom communicated through sacred myth is
untouched by banal questions of historicity. As Keetoowah
Cherokee theologian Randy Woodley points out, "Myth is not
about whether something is fact or fiction; myth is more about
truth. Good myth, according to the adage, is about something that
continues to be true again and again."[1] But fundamentalism that
bows at the altar of empiricism misses all this. When fundamentalism is the dominant paradigm, it's all too easy to suddenly
careen from Christian fundamentalism to atheistic fundamentalism. Sometimes biblical literalism and angry atheism are just
two sides of the same fundamentalist coin.

A few years ago, the pastor of an evangelical-fundamentalist
church not too far from me announced on the Sunday after Easter
that he had become an atheist.[2] (Ironically, in the Revised Common
Lectionary, the Gospel reading for that Sunday is the story of
doubting Thomas and his empirical protest, "Unless I see . . . I will
not believe" [Jn 20:25].) The pastor told his stunned congregation
that he had been an atheist for over a year and that all attempts to
revive his faith had failed. So on the Sunday after Easter, he publicly left Christianity and moved on with his life—a life with no
more Easters.

A few days after his bombshell resignation, I met with this now erstwhile pastor. As I listened to his story, it became apparent that he had not so much lost his faith in historic Christianity as he had lost his credulity for modern fundamentalism. Sadly, he had been formed in a tradition in which Christianity and fundamentalism were so tightly bound together that he could not make a distinction between them. When he jettisoned fundamentalism, Christian faith went with it. For this fundamentalist pastor, if the Bible wasn't literally, historically, and scientifically factual in a biblicist-empiricist sense, then Christianity was a falsity he had to reject. When his fundamentalist house of cards collapsed, it took his Christian faith down with it. In one remarkable leap of faith, a fundamentalist became a newly minted atheist. I did my best to explain to him that he had made the modern mistake of confusing historic Christian faith with early-twentieth-century fundamentalism, but by then, the damage was done and it appears his faith has suffered a fatal blow.

This story I've briefly related is true, but it's also a postmodern parable. By misinterpreting the Enlightenment and the corresponding rise of empiricism as an existential threat to the Christian faith, many frightened Christians sequestered themselves in panic rooms of certitude. But this kind of darkness breeds monsters. Most doubts—like all monsters—are not that scary in the daylight. Most Christians can deal with inevitable doubts as long as there is room for doubt. But when a system is enforced that leaves no room for doubt, benign uncertainties can mutate into faith-destroying monsters. When doubts are locked away in a closet of secrecy, they can grow into formidable ogres.

As a pastor, I've seen it happen. When it's six literal days of creation and a six-thousand-year-old universe or bust—sometimes faith goes bust. I've seen fear-based Christian parents place their children in fundamentalist Christian schools for the sole purpose of shielding little Timmy from the "lies of secular science," only to see Timmy become an atheist before he's out of high school. When you force Timmy to choose between fundamentalist believism and peer-reviewed science, Timmy may not always be persuaded by the pseudo-apologetics from fundamentalist answer men like Ken Ham. I've seen it happen. I've seen too many Christians lose battles they never needed to fight. Like Don Quixote, they imagine harmless windmills as threatening giants and fight a needless battle only to have the windmill-imagined-as-giant prevail. The culture wars have created these kinds of quixotic crusades—and sometimes the tragic outcome is pastors announcing their atheism on the Sunday after Easter.

These days I have a simple mission statement: to help make Christianity possible for my grandchildren and their generation. I want my eight grandchildren to be able to celebrate Easter for a lifetime. And if my grandchildren are to be able to embrace Easter with any kind of authentic faith when they're adults, I cannot afford to ignore their inevitable doubts or try to strong-arm them into unquestioning certitude. In our secular age, that is a formula for atheism. Instead, I do my best to nurture my grandchildren in the rich soil of historic Christian faith, which in its healthiest forms has always been comfortable with mystery and nuance, metaphor and allegory, candid questions and honest doubt. Because in the end, Christianity has suffered more casualties from faux faith than from honest doubt.

In seeking to pass on Christian faith to my grandchildren, I am more interested in presenting to them a beautiful mystery than a collection of ironclad certitudes. If Jesus is presented as beautiful and mysterious as we find him in the Gospels, I'm willing to trust in that beauty to win hearts. It's been said that no one ever became a Christian because they lost an argument. I suspect this is true. I also suspect far more people than we imagine have become converts to Christianity for the simple reason they were charmed by the beauty of Christ. I would much rather ground Christian faith on the beauty of Christ than on biblical literalism. Biblical literalism can be debunked by a college freshman, but the beauty of Christ can withstand the most formidable attack Nietzsche can muster. If I'm hedging my bets on the survival of the Christian faith as we hurdle into a secular age, it's because the King of hearts is still so beautiful. I'm willing to bet my grandchildren's faith on the beauty of Christ. When we adopt the ridiculous dualism of Christ versus science locked in a battle to the death, we are taking a foolish and completely unnecessary risk. From the very beginning, Christians have understood that faith and reason are not rivals but compatible ways of engaging with the mystery of being. A thousand years ago, Saint Anselm gave us the phrase "faith seeking understanding," and the phrase still has currency. Advances in cosmology and quantum physics have only increased our sense of mystery, thus inviting faith to join the conversation.

DEMOLITION OF RESTORATION?

I don't mean to suggest that there aren't real challenges to sustaining a vibrant Christian faith throughout a lifetime. I fully understand the need to rethink and to adjust course in our faith journey. I've had my own experience with this. In midlife, I discovered that the Christianity I knew was too weak and too thin, too compromised with consumerism and too accommodating to Americanism. To sustain a vibrant Christian faith, I had to find a Christianity worthy of the Christ whose name it bears. The good news is that such Christianity exists. It's always existed—though rarely is it the dominant expression of Christianity. Sometimes we have to go on a theological journey to find a faith that can endure for a lifetime.

In my forties, I made the faith-saving discovery that Jesus can turn weak, watered-down Christianity into rich, robust, intoxicating Christianity. I describe my experience as my water-to-wine journey. I know what it is to let go of anti-intellectual theology, doom-oriented eschatology, ticket-to-heaven soteriology, hyper-individualized ecclesiology and discover that something far, *far* better had been there all along. Ever since my initial encounter with Christ as a teenager, I instinctively knew that Jesus was the beauty that saves the world. What I faced in midlife wasn't a deficiency in Jesus but a falseness that marred the beauty of Christ.

Think of an ancient icon of Christ.[3] Imagine that a thousand-year-old *Christ Pantocrator* painted on a wooden panel is discovered in some forgotten monastery. The image of Christ is there, but it's covered with a thick layer of grime, dirt, and soot that has accumulated over centuries and has nearly obliterated the image of Christ. Now imagine that a restoration artist is given the task of returning the icon to its original vibrancy and beauty. Think about how the restoration artist goes about her work. Among her tools for art restoration, we will find brushes and solvents, but we won't find a sledgehammer or explosives. We can't restore art with the same tools we use to demolish a parking garage. Demolition is easy—any fool can do it. But restoration requires wisdom, knowledge, respect, and patience.

Christianity in the twenty-first century may be like a lost icon found in a forgotten monastery. Christian faith has indeed been distorted over the centuries by layers of varnish, lacquer, dirt, and grime. The beautiful image of Christ has been obscured by the imposition of cultural assumptions, political agendas, distorted doctrines, and the corrupting influence of empire. Fundamentalism, literalism, nationalism, and consumerism have created layers of varnish that distort the beautiful image of Christ. But as we seek to remove these contaminants and recover the beauty of Christ, we cannot employ cynical and violent methods. If we do, we run the risk of destroying the priceless treasure in the process. We must be patient and reverent. If all we want to do is deconstruct and destroy the Christian faith, we can swing an angry sledgehammer or burn it all down. But if we want to restore Christian faith, patience and gentleness of wisdom are required.

In our passion to rescue the Christian faith from its myriad of distortions, we are not like the Taliban blowing up the Buddhas of Bamiyan but like the artists who restored Michelangelo's vandalized *Pietà*. In rethinking Christianity, we must always keep in mind that we are handling something enormously precious: faith in Christ. It's precisely because faith in Christ is so precious that we—those who hope to hold on to Christian faith—are committed to the difficult task of restoring it to its original beauty. Thus we cannot use cheap cynicism and crude mockery in this delicate task. We go about it patiently, reverently, gently, always showing deep respect for what has sustained Christian faith and practice for two thousand years.

As you might guess, deconstruction is not my favorite way of talking about making critical adjustments to faith and theology. Deconstruction is a term given to us by the twentieth-century French philosopher Jacques Derrida. Deconstruction theory stresses the limitedness or impossibility of ever arriving at a final interpretation of a text, since words, according to Derrida, are signs pointing to signs. (Though as a Christian, I would appeal to the eternal fixedness of the divine Logos.) Philosopher of religion John Caputo describes Derrida's deconstruction:

> Whenever deconstruction finds a nutshell—a secure axiom or pithy maxim—the very idea is to disturb this tranquility. Indeed, that is a good rule of thumb in deconstruction. *That* is what deconstruction is all about, its very meaning and mission, if it has any. One might even say that cracking nutshells is what deconstruction *is*. In a nutshell.[4]

For Derrida, a text can be endlessly deconstructed because there is no such thing as genuine fixed meaning. And though Derrida does alert us to the possibility of hidden motives that may lurk in a text (often having to do with bids for power), do we really want to spend our whole life endlessly cracking nutshells? As Caputo shrewdly points out, even deconstruction can be deconstructed. And besides, we can't deconstruct forever and have anything left. In the end, we need to have a reason to get out of bed in the morning. Or as René Girard said in a conversation about Derrida's deconstruction theory, "I still believe words mean something." Cornel West says, "The major shortcoming of Derrida's deconstruction project is that it puts a premium on a sophisticated ironic consciousness that tends to preclude and foreclose analyses that guide action with purpose."[5]

Deconstruction seems to be a methodology that has no real endgame. At times, it feels like an invitation to endless cynicism. If as Christians, all we do is deconstruct, we eventually wind up in a world without any more Easters. And a world without Easter is a world without hope—a world on the precipice of nihilism. If the story of a pastor testifying to his atheism on the Sunday after Easter is a postmodern parable, I have another true story that is also a postmodern parable. And it happened on that day that Jacques Derrida died.

3

THE DAY DERRIDA DIED

I was in Paris on the day Jacques Derrida died. Paris was where the founder of deconstruction theory lived, taught, and wrote for over fifty years. Unlike in America where philosophers are resolutely ignored in popular culture, in France, groundbreaking philosophers are still well-known, and the death of this important thinker was headline news. I was in Paris to preach in a church and teach in a Bible college for a few days. Earlier in the week, I had visited Notre Dame where I saw an announcement that on Saturday night, there would be a multimedia presentation in English on the history of this great Gothic cathedral. Ever since my first visit to Paris a decade earlier, and especially after reading Ken Follett's *Pillars of the Earth*, I had been fascinated with Notre Dame. So on Saturday evening, I took the train from the north of Paris into the city center to attend the event. Arriving early, I decided to visit the English-language bookstore Shakespeare and Company located on the Left Bank just across the river from Notre Dame. This famous bookstore was the haunt of Lost Generation literary elites such as Ernest Hemingway, James Joyce, Ezra Pound, and E. E. Cummings. I went to the bookstore to pick up some reading material and was looking in the section that had the Russian masters—Tolstoy, Dostoevsky, Chekhov, and so forth. I found what I was looking for and purchased a paperback copy of Dostoevsky's *The Idiot*.

The Idiot was published in 1868 and was Dostoevsky's attempt to create a perfect soul in the character of Prince Myshkin, a young man so immune to the conniving aspirations of Russian high society that he is called an idiot forty-five times throughout the novel. But Prince Myshkin is not an idiot; he is simply a man motivated by altruistic love instead of class-conscious ambition. In the novel, people call Myshkin an idiot while talking about him among other members of the snobbish St. Petersburg elite, but when they are alone with the prince, they sense his genuine humility and selfless compassion and seem to love being in his presence. Dostoevsky's Prince Myshkin is, in fact, a Christ figure. Strangely, the most famous line in the novel comes from a passage that is utterly irrelevant to the development of the plot. At a party, the young and suicidal nihilist Ippolit Terentyev mockingly says, "'Is it true, Prince, that you once said 'beauty' would save the world? Gentlemen,' he cried loudly to them all, 'the prince insists that beauty will save the world! . . . What beauty will save the world? . . . Are you a zealous Christian? Koyla says you call yourself a Christian.'"[1]

Reportedly, Prince Myshkin has said, "beauty will save the world." In the overall development of the novel, this is a very insignificant thing, but from the moment *The Idiot* was published, Dostoevsky's enigmatic phrase "beauty will save the world" captured the imagination of thinkers, philosophers, and theologians around the world. In 1970, Aleksandr Solzhenitsyn was awarded the Nobel Prize for literature. In his Nobel lecture, Solzhenitsyn said that "beauty will save the world" was not a careless phrase from Dostoevsky but a prophecy. When Dostoevsky introduced "beauty will save the world" into the lexicon of religious and philosophical thought through the character of Prince Myshkin, he was clearly pointing us to the beauty of Christ.

This was the book I purchased in Paris on the day Derrida died. The odd thing about my purchase of *The Idiot* at Shakespeare and Company is that I already had a lovely hardback Everyman's Library edition of *The Idiot*—in my hotel room! I paid twelve euros for the paperback edition, thinking I would have an hour to read it before I got back to the hotel. I'll admit that it seemed a bit extravagant at the time, but it turned out that I *needed* to have that book with me.

Having purchased my paperback *Idiot*, I walked across the bridge from the Left Bank to Notre Dame for the hour-long presentation covering the nine-hundred-year history of the cathedral. Although the program was mostly about the design and construction of Notre Dame, it began with a brief biography of Saint Denis, the third-century martyr and first bishop of Paris who was beheaded in 275. I was deeply moved by both the heroic courage of Saint Denis and the devotion of those who labored for a lifetime in the construction of Notre Dame, knowing that they would not live to see its completion. Both the first bishop of Paris and Notre Dame's stonemasons lived for something that would outlive them. The multimedia presentation was attended by a few dozen English-speaking tourists, and it wasn't particularly religious. Nevertheless, at the end of the program, I bowed my head in the massive Gothic cathedral and prayed a simple prayer: "God, use me more in Paris."

Leaving Notre Dame, I got on the train and continued reading *The Idiot*. At the first stop, a young man sat down opposite me. After a few moments, he said, "That's a great book you're reading." Looking up, I asked if he'd read *The Idiot*, and he said he was reading it right now. We both thought that was an interesting coincidence.

We began to talk about literature and philosophy, and at one point, the death of Derrida came up, so we talked for a few minutes about deconstruction theory. The young man was Asian, and his name was Yu. He had just graduated from college and was backpacking across Europe. I never found out exactly where he was from, but by his accent, I think he may have been from Singapore. When I asked Yu about his studies, he told me he had earned a double degree in political science and history. I remarked on how that was a good combination of degrees because political science is the study of the human attempt at self-governance and history is the record of our failures. He laughed and agreed. Yu was obviously an intelligent and motivated young man, so I asked him a pointed question.

"Yu, with what you know about politics and history, what hope do you have for the world?"

He replied, "Oh, I don't have any hope for the world."

I told him that seemed quite sad.

Yu was quiet for a moment and then said, "I've heard that Fyodor Dostoevsky was a Christian. Do you know anything about that?"

I replied, "As a matter of fact, I do."

Then I told Yu how Dostoevsky had been raised in an Orthodox Christian home, but that during his high school years, he had become an agnostic. After college and a brief stint as a military engineer, Dostoevsky was pursuing a writing career in St. Petersburg where he joined a secret literary society critical of czarist Russia. When he was twenty-seven, Dostoevsky and five other members of the secret society were arrested for treason and sentenced to death. After eight months in prison, the young writer and his companions were taken from the Peter and Paul Fortress to the Semyonovsky Parade Ground for what he thought would be his execution. Emperor Nikolai changed the sentence but ordered that the reprieve be announced only at the last moment. The condemned prisoners were taken to the parade ground, blindfolded, tied to posts in front of the firing squad, and just before the command to fire was given, a horseman galloped in announcing that the emperor had commuted their sentence to four years of hard labor and four years of exile in Siberia.

Dostoevsky was immediately clamped in irons, put in an open sleigh in the dead of winter, and taken away to a brutal prison camp in Omsk—a journey of two thousand miles! As Dostoevsky was entering the Siberian prison that he would later describe as "the house of the dead," a woman gave him a copy of the Gospels. During the four years of his imprisonment, the only reading material this highly literate man had was the Gospels' accounts of the life of Jesus Christ. He read these Gospels over and over. John was his favorite. I've seen this well-worn book in the Dostoevsky museum in St. Petersburg. Like Aleksandr Solzhenitsyn a century later, it was during his prison years that Dostoevsky came to believe that Jesus Christ is indeed the Savior of the world.

This is the story I told to Yu on the train in Paris on the day that Derrida died.

After hearing about Dostoevsky's faith in Christ, Yu asked, "What do you do?"

"I'm a pastor."

Yu was surprised by this. After a moment of pensive silence, Yu leaned close and whispered, "Since you're a pastor, I want to tell you something. I grew up in a Christian home, but in high school, I became an atheist. Today I went to Notre Dame, just to see the Gothic architecture, not to pray. But when I walked into the cathedral and saw the beauty, I knew I was wrong; I know God exists. I tried to pray. I tried to tell God that I was sorry, but I don't think God heard my prayer because I walked away from him all those years ago."

I said, "Yu, now let me tell you something. God *did* hear your prayer! I just came from Notre Dame and I too prayed there—I prayed for God to use me more in Paris. God heard both of our prayers and is answering both prayers right now. This evening I bought this paperback copy of *The Idiot*, even though I have a nice hardcover copy in my hotel room. I needed to have it so you would see it, and we would have our conversation about Derrida and Dostoevsky and Jesus and how the beauty of Christ will save the world."

Tears came to Yu's eyes. I asked Yu if he had read the Bible. He said he had not. I suggested that he read the Gospel of John—Dostoevsky's favorite. Yu said he would. Then I asked Yu if he would like me to pray for him. He said yes, and so I prayed that Yu would find in Jesus Christ the saving hope for the world—just like Dostoevsky did. As we finished praying, I looked up and the train was at my stop. I said, "Yu, I have to go," and got off the train.

That's the true story of Yu and me on the train in Paris on the day that Derrida died. I never learned Yu's last name or even where he was from. We were just two passengers on the same train. We had both been to Notre Dame that day. We were both reading *The Idiot*. We had half an hour's conversation inspired by a fictional Christ figure that some people thought was an idiot. There was a miracle on that train. Because we had, quite unintentionally though providentially, gathered around Jesus Christ, we were not alone. For as Jesus said, "Where two or three are gathered in my name, there I am among them" (Mt 18:20). Yes, I do not doubt that Jesus was with Yu and me on that train in Paris on the day that deconstruction died. And I'm sure Yu knew it as well.

OUR LADY ON FIRE

I've told this story as a postmodern parable for years, but now it has a poignant postscript. It was Monday of Holy Week 2019 and I had just finished leading a noontime prayer service when I heard the awful news that Notre Dame was on fire. *Our Lady was on fire!* I turned on the television and watched in horror for the next three hours. I hadn't felt like this since 9/11. I wept. Millions of us did. The French news magazine *Paris Match* said, "Today, they weep for her in every language."

Like millions of others, I watched in real time what seemed to be the agonizing death of a priceless treasure. For me, the most dreadful moment came when the 750-ton spire, already engulfed in flames, finally collapsed. It marked the moment when we all feared Notre Dame would be forever lost. "Notre-Dame had always seemed eternal, and the medieval builders certainly thought it would last until the Day of Judgment; but suddenly we saw that it could be destroyed."[2] As I looked at Notre Dame on television, everything was on fire, and what hope for its salvation could there be now?

I love Paris. I think the City of Lights is the most beautiful in the world. But when I am there I have a palpable sense of its deep secularity. Yes, the medieval cathedrals are still present, but contemporary faith seems pushed to the extreme periphery. Paris is arguably the epicenter of modern atheism and Western secularism. It's the home of the Enlightenment, the French Revolution, Voltaire, Baron d'Holbach, and Jean-Paul Sartre. Modern Parisians walking with shoulder-shrugging indifference past Notre Dame day after day could be an apt metaphor for the state of Christianity in a secular age. But as night fell on April 15, 2019, the people of Paris gathered in front of the still-burning cathedral and held a candlelight vigil for Our Lady. There was no cheering, no one gloated, no one shouted "good riddance," and no one tweeted "empty the pews" or "burn it all down." Instead, "television cameras showed thousands of grief-stricken faces lit by the flames, some singing hymns, others just weeping as they watched the beautiful cathedral burn."[3] I suspect many Parisians didn't know how much they loved their cathedral until they saw it in flames. It would be easy to take Notre Dame for granted, even to ignore her, and yet still assume she would always be there if you ever decided you wanted to visit her. Buildings burn every day, but most of them don't cause the world to weep. A factory on fire is not the same as a cathedral on fire; Walmart in flames is not the same as Notre Dame in flames. In a secular age suspicious of the sacred, we still know deep down that some things really are sacred. But sometimes, we don't know how sacred they are until they're on fire. As Joni Mitchell sang:

Don't it always seem to go
That you don't know what you've got
'Till it's gone
They paved paradise
And put up a parking lot[4]

I suspect that many Parisians didn't know how beloved their cathedral was until they saw it in flames, and I also suspect that many who think they are done with Christianity may not be as done as they suppose—at least not when they see Our Lady on fire. Most people have a deep-seated instinct that we *don't* want to live in a world devoid of a community that is at least trying to preserve the beauty of Jesus. We may critique the church. Some may be done with the church. Others in their anger may shout "empty the pews!" But do we really think the world would be a better place without the story of Jesus? Do we really want to rid the world of the Beatitudes, the Sermon on the Mount, and the parable of the prodigal son? Do we really think that the world would be better off without Christmas and Easter? Do we honestly think that our own lives will be better if we burn our Christian faith to the ground? This is not the kind of deconstruction that leads to a better world or a better life. Paris is *not* better without Notre Dame, and the world is *not* better without Christianity.

Thankfully, our worst fears were not realized. Notre Dame was not entirely lost; our Lady did not perish in those awful flames on Holy Monday, but it came close. The *New York Times* reported that the cathedral came within twenty minutes of being lost.[5] Notre Dame was saved only because a team of firefighters volunteered to carry firehoses up the spiral staircases of the burning bell towers after another team had refused because of the danger. Through the heroic actions of firefighters who risked their lives for the beloved cathedral, the towers did not collapse, and Notre Dame was saved. It was severely damaged, but not forever lost.

One of the most iconic photos of the Notre Dame fire was taken from inside the cathedral the morning after the blaze. In the foreground, we see charred beams from the collapsed roof lying between the pew benches and the altar. On the high altar, we see a marble statue of the Virgin Mary holding the lifeless body of Christ after his crucifixion. Above the marble statue is a large golden cross that is reflecting the light and seems to stand triumphant above the wreckage. Behind the cross, the stained-glass windows at the east end of the cathedral are aglow with the sunrise. The photograph bears testimony to the reality of the catastrophe, but on the whole, it brims with hope. In the night everything was on fire, but in the dawn Our Lady still stands, the cross still shines, and rays of hope still illuminate a sacred place.

What can we do when everything is on fire? Perhaps we can recognize that not all structures of belief are the same. Some deserve to be condemned, some need to be deconstructed, and some are not worth saving. But other structures of belief are worth risking everything to try to save them. Yu's faith got a second chance when he visited Notre Dame on the day that Derrida died. A cathedral that can do something like that is worth saving, and the world is grateful to those firefighters who risked their lives to do so. If a cathedral inspired by and built to the glory of the Christian faith is worth saving, how much more is *the faith itself* worth saving?

If you're going through a time of deconstruction, maybe it's worth trying to save that which is precious before you let it all burn down. Maybe it's worth trying to separate the wheat from the chaff before you launch into a world without anymore Easters. Deconstruction doesn't have to mean demolition. I'm convinced that the beautiful cathedral of Christian faith that has stood for two millennia and has helped flood the world with the message of Jesus is worth trying to save. Renovate what needs to be renovated, throw out what needs to be thrown out, deconstruct what needs to be deconstructed, and even let some of it burn, but don't burn it *all* down. The cathedral of Christian faith, Our Lady, who has nurtured and carried the gospel message of Jesus Christ, is worth our best efforts to save. Seeing the Cathedral of Notre Dame on a spring day while strolling along the Left Bank in Paris reminds me that Christian faith can still enact a beautiful presence in our world.

◆　◆　◆

It was one of those spring days that is so gentle and pretty that all of Paris treats it like a Sunday, crowding the squares and the boulevards. During such days of clear skies, warmth, and peace, there comes a supreme moment at which to appreciate the portal of Notre Dame. It is when the sun, already sinking, shines almost directly on the cathedral. Its rays, more and more horizontal, slowly leave the pavement and climb the vertical façade to highlight the countless carvings against their shadows, until the great rose window, like the eye of the cyclops, is reddened as if by reflections from a furnace.

VICTOR HUGO, *THE HUNCHBACK OF NOTRE DAME*[6]

THE END IS
THE BEGINNING

The he pivotal event of my life occurred when I was quite young, only a teenager. At the precarious age of fifteen, when I was beginning to head down some destructive roads, Jesus Christ captured my heart with holy fascination. I can relate the events of my sudden spiritual awakening, but all these years later, I still don't understand *why* it happened. At a significant crossroads early in life, why was the course of my entire life suddenly changed by an encounter with Jesus Christ? I don't know; it remains a mystery. I *do* know that at the center of my faith, there is found not a religion or a book or a theology but a person—the crucified and risen Lord Jesus Christ. Before I ever read a theological book and even before I had read the Bible in a serious way, I came to believe that Jesus Christ is the Son of God, the Savior of the world. Why? The only explanation I can give is to say with the apostle Paul that God was "pleased to reveal his Son to me" (Gal 1:15-16). I confess this, but I can't prove it. I can't prove that God revealed his Son to me; neither can it be disproved—I can only testify to it and let others decide whether or not my witness is credible.

However, I cannot deny the burning witness of my heart. Like John Wesley, I too have felt my heart strangely warmed by the risen Son of God. The center of the human being is the heart—not the mind. I didn't think my way to faith, rather I encountered Christ with my heart. Ultimately, the witness of my heart is as credible as the reasonings of my mind. And if you say the heart can be deceived, I will say the mind can also be deceived. A pure heart can be trusted. As Jesus said, "Blessed are the pure in heart, for they will see God" (Mt 5:8). My conversion was mystical, not rational. But that does not make it any less credible. As Blaise Pascal famously said, "The heart has its reasons of which reason knows nothing."[1] When it comes to placing my faith in Jesus, I'm following my heart. If my heart has deceived me regarding Jesus Christ, then it is the most beautiful deception of all. But I can't believe that the most beautiful story of all is born of a lie.

The perception of true beauty (not mere prettification) is as reliable a guide to profound truth as reason is. My experience is that beauty is a more reliable guide than reason. Voltaire, the caustic Enlightenment critic of Christianity, once said, "If God did not exist it would be necessary to invent him."[2] But I say if Jesus Christ did not exist, we would never have imagined him. Who would have imagined that billions of people would eventually come to worship God as a crucified Jew? The gospel exists not because it was invented but because it happened. The most astounding thing I know about the gospel is that being disguised under the disfigurement of an ugly crucifixion and death, Christ on the cross is paradoxically the clearest revelation of who God is. And I can't imagine any news that is better than the good news that God is like Jesus. Some things in the universe are too good *not* to be true.

YOUR THEOLOGICAL HOUSE

My lifelong journey with Jesus began with a mystical experience, but it was of course necessary to construct a theological house around Jesus. My theological house, by which I mean theology, is how I think and speak about the God revealed in Christ. My theological house is the palace in my mind for Christ the King. The theological house is important, but only because it is the palace of the King, and we must never forget that the King and the palace are not synonymous. In other words, the center of Christian faith is not theology but Christ. That is not to say that our theological house is unimportant or unnecessary. In fact, our theological house is not only important but is also inevitable. Any attempt to think or speak about God revealed in Christ is to engage in theological construction. Thus we all have a theological house—some of it we inherit and some of it we construct ourselves. Our theological house is not Jesus but the space that Jesus inhabits in our thought and speech. Our theological house can be helpful and enhancing, worthy of our King, or it can be inadequate, possibly injurious, and unworthy of our King.

After my initial encounter with Christ, I began to construct my theological house. Every time I formed an opinion about God or dared to assert that God was a certain way, I was building my theology—even if I was almost entirely unaware of doing this. I didn't think of myself as constructing a theology. I simply thought, *these are the things that I know about God* (whether they were true or not). I was mostly unaware that my theological house was a composite of ancient traditions and modern fancies, faithful orthodoxies and aberrant fallacies. I acquired the building materials for my theological house from various sources—the Baptist church of my childhood, the Jesus movement and charismatic renewal of the 1970s, and whatever popular preachers and teachers I happened to embrace. For twenty-five years or so, my theological house was, shall we say, adequate. Or so I thought.

Around the age of forty, I began to be aware of certain inadequacies in my theological house. It was generally too small, mostly too impoverished, and altogether too informed by the garish style of modern fundamentalism. Jesus was still living in my theological house where I worshiped him as King, but I was living with my King in an unworthy construct—a theology that was too characterized by sectarian certitude, Western individualism, American consumerism, and religious nationalism. I never doubted Jesus, but I began to have serious doubts about the theological house I had built around Jesus.

In fall 2003 I reached the place where I said, "I can't live in this house anymore." I held on to Jesus, but my dilapidated house was becoming uninhabitable. I was afraid it was going to be condemned. I was too embarrassed by my theological house to invite company into it. I wasn't ashamed of Jesus, but the theological house I had built around Jesus had become an embarrassment. Theories of eschatology, theories of atonement, and theories of final judgment I had inherited or picked up along the way now seemed to clash with the beauty of Christ. An unavoidable eschatological megawar in the Middle East, the cross as the Father's violent anger inflicted on his Son, hell as God's eternal torture chamber—these theological ideas had become too ugly to be endured. Something had to be done. The saving grace was that I was able to make the critical distinction between Jesus Christ and my theological house. Jesus Christ is the same yesterday, today, and forever, but my theological house was not. It was clear that my theological house could *not* remain the same yesterday, today, and forever. It was a time for a major remodeling project!

In 2004, I embarked on a massive theological renovation. I didn't want to demolish my faith; I wanted to restore it. It involved a lot of praying, reading, rethinking, and engaging with new voices, both ancient and modern. It was an exciting time, though it was not easy. Remodeling my house *while I was still living in it* was a messy and disruptive thing! The remodeling of my theological house was like every remodeling project—it was much more complicated, it took far longer, and was more costly than I estimated. But it was worth it all!

When I speak of renovating a theological house, it should be understood that a theological house is not one thing. It's not a one-room bungalow; a theological house is more like a rambling mansion with dozens of rooms. Some of the rooms in my theological house were largely untouched. Some rooms were only slightly remodeled. But some rooms were too dilapidated to be salvaged—they had to be torn down. A fresh coat of paint would not do, instead the sledgehammer was brought in. I embarked on the massive remodel of my theological house when I reached the point where I had no other choice. I believed in Jesus, but in midlife I became aware of how much of my theology was incongruent with the one who was the true object of my faith. I was willing to sacrifice my theology for my Lord.

The eschatology I had inherited from modern dispensationalism and the rapture theology that dominated popular evangelicalism comprised an entire wing of my theological house and none of it was salvageable—it all had to be subjected to theological deconstruction. Many parts of my theological house only needed renovating, but the eschatology had to be razed. Thanks to help from credible scholars such as N. T. Wright, Barbara Rossing, and Richard Bauckham, I was able to quickly demolish the hyperviolent, doom-oriented, escapist-fiction eschatology set forth in books like *The Late Great Planet Earth* and The Left Behind series and replace it with an eschatology that is theologically sound and worthy of the Prince of Peace. I can say that in the remodeling of my theological house, my Christology was almost untouched, my soteriology was remodeled, and my eschatology was completely replaced.

Though *deconstruction* is not my preferred term for the process of making needed theological adjustments, indeed some of my theological transition did involve deconstruction. These aspects of deconstruction didn't come from a place of anger or cynicism but from a quest for truth and beauty. To the extent that my spiritual growth has involved some deconstruction, I can say that it was a deconstruction that led to the new construction of a more beautiful theology. Today, my theological house, though never entirely complete, is a comfortable place to live, and I'm no longer embarrassed by it. More importantly, my theological house today is more worthy of Christ the King.

During the remodel of my theological house, I had to trust the Holy Spirit to be the contractor. The Spirit led me to the right books, the right friends, the right prayers. When I asked how much this remodel would cost me, the Spirit let me know I had to put everything in escrow and trust her with it. Several times during the remodel I was afraid that all was lost and coming to an ugly end. But that's not what happened. It turns out that it was all part of the process that led to a beautiful renovation. I was being born again again, and the end was the beginning. That's my story, but Mary Magdalene has a similar story.

MARY MAGDALENE: THE APOSTLE TO THE APOSTLES

Mary Magdalene was a woman of means who came from Magdala, the largest and most prosperous fishing village on the Sea of Galilee. She was among the wealthy and influential Galilean women who financially supported the itinerate ministry of Jesus and his disciples. Among these female patrons we find Joanna, the wife of Chuza, the business manager for King Herod. Obviously, we shouldn't imagine these women as simple peasants. Though Christian iconography tends to depict Mary as a young woman, there is no indication that this was the case, and circumstantial evidence leads us to think she was probably an older woman, maybe owning her own business and possibly a widow. And it should be made clear that Mary Magdalene was not a prostitute! This unfortunate legend largely came into existence due to a sermon preached by Gregory the Great in 591, where he mistakenly conflated Mary Magdalene with the unnamed woman "who was a sinner" found in Luke 7.

Though not a prostitute, Mary Magdalene was a troubled soul. Both Mark and Luke tell us that Jesus had driven seven demons out of her. What form Mary's demonic troubles took we don't know; what we do know is that after meeting Jesus and being healed of her demons she became his most faithful follower. Mary followed Jesus through Galilee. She followed him to Jerusalem. She was with him at his crucifixion when the disciples were absent. She was with him at his burial. She was the first person to encounter the risen Christ and the first to proclaim the resurrection. It is rightly said that Mary was the apostle to the apostles. Other than Mary the mother of Jesus, Mary Magdalene is the most important woman in the New Testament. Because all four Gospels name Mary Magdalene as a witness to the resurrection, Cynthia Bourgeault emphasizes the significance:

> Given the shifting sands of oral history, the unanimity of this testimony is astounding. It suggests that among the earliest Christians the stature of Mary Magdalene is of the highest order of magnitude—more so than even the Virgin Mother (mentioned as present at the crucifixion in only one gospel and in none at the resurrection). Mary Magdalene's place of honor is so strong that even the heavy hand of a later, male-dominated ecclesiology cannot entirely dislodge it.[3]

Mary's Easter encounter with Jesus in the garden of Joseph of Arimathea is one of the most poignant stories in the Gospels. She may have been Jesus' most faithful follower, yet even she was not prepared for Jesus to be killed. Like all of the other followers, Mary was waiting for Jesus to be crowned king, not crowned with thorns. But Mary was a witness to all the horrors of Jesus' passion. After seeing the crucifixion, death, and burial of her beloved Teacher, Mary entered the dark night of the bitter end. The Jesus she had known and loved was dead. Hers was the ultimate dark night of the soul, a most brutal deconstruction of faith. But it's not the end of the story.

Early on the first day of the week, while it was still dark, Mary Magdalene came to the tomb (Jn 20:1). The dawn had not yet come and Mary was still in the dark night of deconstruction so severe that everything seemed to be lost. In the darkness of her despair Mary came as a mourner to the tomb of Jesus, the place of the final dissolution of the faith she had held. But what Mary supposed was the end was in fact a new beginning. A dark night of deconstruction *can* be followed by a new dawn of renewed faith. At the inexplicably empty tomb, Mary met a Jesus she did not recognize—a stranger she supposed was the gardener. It was only as he spoke her name that Mary recognized the gardener as Jesus.

> Jesus said to her, "Woman, why are you weeping? Whom are you seeking?" Supposing him to be the gardener, she said to him, "Sir, if you have carried him away, tell me where you have laid him, and I will take him away." Jesus said to her, "Mary." She turned and said to him in Aramaic, "Rabboni!" (which means Teacher). Jesus said to her, "Do not cling to me, for I have not yet ascended to the Father." (Jn 20:15-17 ESV)

Jesus tells Mary not to cling to him. Why? The answer is related to Jesus' ascension. Mary has to stop clinging to the Jesus she had previously known—a Jesus confined to the ordinary limits of time and space—and learn to know him as the one who now "fill all things everywhere with himself" (Eph 1:23 NLT). Mary Magdalene had to stop clinging to the Jesus she had known in the past in order to recognize the risen Christ who would be present to her now and forever. The risen Christ that Mary meets in the garden is not a different person from the one she had met in Galilee, *but he must now be known in a different way.* Mary had known the historical Jesus—the Jesus who is now forever locked within a particular historical time and place. But she could not forever cling to the historical Jesus.[4]

After his ascension, Mary must know Jesus not as the historical figure who walked through Galilee but as the risen and ascended Christ who now fills the cosmos with his saving presence. Mary cannot cling to the historical Jesus, she must reach out to the ascended Christ. Is this a lesser knowing of Jesus? No! Remember, the apostle Paul never knew the historical Jesus, yet no one has given us a greater revelation of Jesus Christ than Paul. The Jesus of history was known by only a small group of people living in Galilee and Judea in the first century, but the risen Christ is accessible to all people everywhere at all times. "The risen Christ is the only man who is in present and perpetual communion with all beings."[5]

THE QUEST FOR THE HISTORICAL JESUS

In 1906, Albert Schweitzer published his groundbreaking book *The Quest of the Historical Jesus,* launching several waves of academic research into the Jesus of history. Other notable scholars connected with historical Jesus research include Ernst Käsemann, Robert Funk, John Dominic Crossan, E. P. Sanders, James Dunn, Marcus Borg, Richard Hayes, and N. T. Wright. I've read a good deal of historical Jesus scholarship and have benefited from it. There is value in knowing as much as we can about Jesus of Nazareth in his historical context. But we have to keep in mind that we can never actually reach the historical Jesus—we cannot travel back in time. The past lies on the other side of an abyss we cannot cross. The Jesus of Nazareth who walked the hills of Galilee in dusty sandals is unreachable.

However, we *can* encounter the Christ that Mary Magdalene met as a gardener beside the empty tomb, the Christ the two disciples met as a stranger on the Emmaus road, the Christ that Saul of Tarsus met in a blinding light on the Damascus road. A historical person is locked within an unreachable past, but the risen and ascended Christ is available to all. Ultimately, we do not have access to the historical Jesus but to the risen Lord. We're not going to find Jesus in an archaeological dig but in the place of prayer and worship.

To initially meet and begin to know Jesus is a wonderful thing. For Mary Magdalene, it meant being set free from seven demons. But even Mary Magdalene could not assume that her first understanding of Jesus captured the fullness of who Jesus is. The Jesus who Mary encountered in the garden far transcended her initial understanding of the Jesus she first knew in Galilee. But in between being delivered from seven demons and meeting the risen Christ in the guise of a gardener was a dark night when all seemed lost. The beauty of Mary's story is that a dark night was only the antecedent to a new dawn where a bitter end became a new beginning.

Like Mary Magdalene, you may reach a place in your faith that feels like a dead end. Or to use my earlier metaphor, you may realize that parts of your theological house may have to undergo some deconstruction as part of a massive remodel. But this doesn't have to be the end of your Christian faith—it *can* lead to a new beginning. The problem is that extraneous doctrines, wrong ideas about God, and wrong attitudes toward culture can become attached to our faith in Jesus. This often occurs in childhood or early in conversion. For a time, these wrong ideas, theologies, and attitudes may cause us no problem, but then something happens that can put our faith in peril. It could be almost anything—discovering that the universe is *not* six thousand years old and that evolution is an overwhelmingly credible scientific theory, a visit to Auschwitz that raises disturbing questions about the pernicious doctrine of eternal conscious torment, or reading a verse in the Bible that says women should keep silent in church and having to admit you don't believe that. Suddenly you're thrown into a crisis of faith, but it doesn't have to be the end. It can be an opportunity to move beyond the literalism, the infernalism, and the biblicism that never were truly compatible with a mature faith in Jesus Christ.

HARD-WON ADVICE

These examples of things that can trigger a crisis of faith are not imaginative but are drawn from my experience as a pastor. I've talked with people whose faith has been threatened by wrong ways of thinking about science, hell, the Bible, and other injurious notions they have picked up along the way. I've been able to help people through these dark crises of faith and into the sun-drenched lands of a reborn faith. So please allow me to share with you five bits of hard-won advice.

Don't be afraid and don't be ashamed. Passing through periods of doubt is a necessary part of spiritual growth and it's nothing to be embarrassed about. Matthew tells us that when the risen Christ met with the apostles on the mountain in Galilee, "they worshiped him; but some doubted" (Mt 28:17). What did they doubt? Did they doubt that it was Jesus? Did they doubt that Jesus was really alive? Did they doubt that they should worship Jesus? Did they doubt their own ability to carry out the task Jesus was giving them? Who knows? We're not told. Some doubted. So what? Their doubt didn't disqualify their faith, and your doubt doesn't have to disqualify your faith. Sometimes doubt is a doorway to better faith.

In my forties, I began to doubt some things. I began to doubt the dispensationalist eschatology I had inherited. I began to doubt the compatibility of a doctrine of eternal conscious torment with the God of love revealed in Jesus Christ. I began to doubt the cozy association between American patriotism and Christianity. I began to doubt the credibility of the consumerist Christianity that was so popular. And all of these were *good* doubts! I was doubting what *should* be doubted. There's a sense in which I can say I doubted my way to a better faith.

Keep in mind that your theological house is not Jesus. When I went through a period of profound theological reassessment—call it deconstruction if you like—I never once feared losing Jesus. I realize this isn't everyone's experience, but for whatever reason I was able to make the vital distinction between my Lord and my theology. I was willing to sacrifice all of my certitude, all my theology, and, if need be, even my vocation to stay on the journey of following Jesus. I could pray, "Jesus, I believe in you even if I don't know exactly what that means or what that's going to look like on the other side of this." My constant was my faith in Jesus Christ as the Son of God. That faith did not have to be tied to any particular eschatology, atonement theory, or speculations about the afterlife.

When I speak with former Christians who have become atheists, I often ask them to describe the God they don't believe in, and almost always I'm able to say, "I don't believe in that God either." If they say, "I can't believe in a God who would eternally torture the vast majority of humanity just because they didn't believe the right things," I say, "I can't believe in *that* God either, and I don't believe *that* God exists." These skeptics aren't actually *intellectual* atheists; they are *protest* atheists. They don't have a *rational* objection to God; they have a *moral* objection to God. They are saying that a God of capricious cruelty should not exist.

And I'm happy to report that such a God *does not* exist. Please realize that you can let go of absurd and heinous doctrines and still hold on to Jesus.

Beware the pendulum. An angry reaction to *everything* in your inherited tradition is probably unwise and unnecessary. You may not need to take a wrecking ball to your entire theological house. Try to move in response to light and love and not in response to anger and resentment. Unless you come from an aberrant or abusive sect, you probably received many treasures from your tradition that are worth cherishing. They may have given you a bad eschatology or an ugly theology of final judgment, but they also told you about the Jesus who forgives sinners and offers abundant life.

Unless you came from a deliberately manipulative cult, your church passed on their wrong ideas about God in good faith—they weren't trying to deceive you but simply didn't know anything better. They were only teaching what they had been taught. If you have been given the grace to see something better, give them grace for the mistakes they couldn't avoid. And here's one more warning about the pendulum phenomenon. When people from a conservative tradition begin to question some tenants of theological conservatism, they often find a way forward through a more progressive theology. But it should not be assumed that a progressive move is in every case the way forward. It's important to understand that progressive fundamentalism is just as false and destructive as conservative fundamentalism. We seek to discover God as revealed in Christ, not in an ism, be it conservative or progressive.

Open up to the whole body of Christ. Those beliefs most in need of deconstruction and remodeling are usually the product of isolated and sectarian camps. The theological dead end you have arrived at may only be a dead end in a relatively small neighborhood in the vast kingdom of Christ. It's highly unlikely that the theological problems you are struggling with are unique to you. It's more likely that Christians have wrestled with similar questions for centuries and that there are dozens of good books to help you navigate your theological conundrum. But you may not find them in your particular denomination or movement. The solution may be to become more ecumenical and try to read more widely. Seek out those regarded as the best thinkers and teachers within various traditions—Eastern Orthodox, Roman Catholic, Anglican, mainline Protestant, Anabaptist, evangelical, and Pentecostal. I've benefited greatly from Orthodox soteriology, Catholic practices of spiritual formation, Anglican liturgy, mainline scholarship, Anabaptist peace studies, evangelical energy, and the Pentecostal emphasis on the Holy Spirit.[6]

Be patient—a new dawn will come. Between the death of Good Friday and the resurrection of Easter Sunday, there is the patient waiting of Holy Saturday. Mary Magdalene saw Jesus die, and she saw Jesus alive again. But in between, she had to wait through a long Holy Saturday. If you wait, you will find Jesus again in a new way. But if you walk away from it all, you may never find Jesus in newness as Mary did. If you are going through deconstruction and hoping to renovate your theological house, remember remodeling projects take a while. No matter what you've been told, it's going to take longer than two weeks.

My water-to-wine theological transition took several years, and it took several years more to bring our church through this transition. Spiritual maturity is found in patience, not in rash actions. The spiritual journey is, of course, always ongoing, but you will not be deconstructing and renovating forever. Be patient, and the day will come when your faith will find a place of newness, peace, and contentment. Remember, Jesus called you, and he will not forsake you. You know his voice that calls you. You know his love that draws you. You can trust that voice and you can trust that love. Be assured that Jesus is leading you to a good place. T. S. Eliot said it this way:

> With the drawing of this Love and the voice of this Calling
> We shall not cease from exploration
> And the end of all our exploring
> Will be to arrive where we started
> And know the place for the first time.[7]

LOSING JESUS

I f in our long journey of faith we reach a place where the
system of belief we have inherited, crafted, and held on to
comes into question because we now see it as naive, contradictory,
bigoted, or maybe just plain false, we may fear that we will lose
Jesus altogether. This is a disturbing thought. If for the sake of
moral and intellectual integrity we are forced to reject what is ugly
and incoherent in a Christian theology, don't we also have to
move beyond Jesus? Isn't Jesus so inseparably bound to Christianity that to profoundly rethink Christianity is to risk losing
Jesus? In answering this question, we need to make a critical distinction between three separate entities: Jesus Christ, the church,
and Christianity.

Christ is the Word of God—the eternal Logos assuming human
flesh in Jesus of Nazareth.

The *church* is the gathered community of the baptized who
confess that Jesus is Lord and believe that Jesus is the truth of God
revealed in human life.

Christianity is the religion of beliefs and practices about Jesus
Christ developed by the church.

To put it as succinctly as possible, Christ is God, the church is a community, and Christianity is a religion. Recognizing that Christianity is a religion helps temper the tendency toward reckless all-or-nothing claims. We should not claim that Christianity is the ultimate truth. Rather, Christianity claims that *Jesus Christ* is the ultimate truth. Of course, Jesus Christ has to be interpreted, and this is the project of the church over time. The conclusions of the church regarding Christ are what we find in Christianity. The church has a consensus regarding the truth of Christ, and this is what we find outlined in the historic creeds.

But there is also deep disagreement within the church regarding how to interpret the totality of truth as revealed in Christ. For example, Catholicism and Calvinism are very different, but both are expressions of Christianity. What they have in common is the essentials regarding the truth of Christ as outlined in the Nicene Creed. Catholics and Calvinists don't need to claim they have absolute truth (and it's better if they don't). It's enough that both Catholics and Calvinists belong to the broad religion of Christianity—a religion that seeks to interpret the truth as revealed in Christ. Within the Christian religion there is room for disagreement on how the truth of God revealed in Christ is to be interpreted. As Christians, we can't believe just *anything* (for example, that Jesus is not God) because that would eventually end with Christianity being *nothing*. But within the broad borders of the historic creeds there is plenty of room for creative theology and rigorous debate.

We get in trouble when we fail to make critical distinctions between Christ, the church, and Christianity. When we conflate these three into a single entity, we are quickly mired in confusion. We see this problem in the popular but sloppy claim that Christianity isn't a religion. If Christianity isn't a religion, then what is it? The most commonly given answer is the trite quip that Christianity is a relationship. But all that does is make Christianity a private matter in which the lone believer is the sole arbiter of truth, and that is a recipe for spiritual disaster. If we want to reduce the risk of such disasters, we need to think more precisely about what we mean by Christ, the church, and Christianity.

Contrary to the popular aphorism, Christianity is not a relationship; it's a religion. (Though we could say that the goal of the Christian religion is relationship with the Holy Trinity.) But what do we mean by religion? Religion is a human construct seeking to understand and encounter the divine. Without shared religion, every person is left to invent their own spirituality. This may appeal to the modern individual whose mantra is "I'm spiritual but not religious," but disdain for received religious tradition is more akin to every individual left to discover the wheel and harness fire on their own. Without shared religion, we cannot build on the spiritual progress achieved by those who have gone before us. Without the wisdom of healthy religion, we consign ourselves to theological ignorance and spiritual poverty. Tradition can and should be constantly reevaluated, but tradition should not be uncritically rejected simply because it's tradition. We need a healthy balance between challenging and preserving tradition. Polish philosopher Leszek Kolakowski says it like this:

> There are two circumstances we should always keep simultaneously in mind: First, if the new generations had not continually revolted against inherited tradition we would still be living in caves; second, if revolt against inherited tradition should become universal, we would soon be back in the caves. . . . A society in which tradition becomes a cult is condemned to stagnation; a society that tries to live entirely through revolt against tradition condemns itself to destruction.[1]

Religion primarily consists of vetted beliefs and traditional practices—beliefs about the divine and practices that help us to encounter the divine. The Great Tradition within Christianity consists of the beliefs and practices that are intended to form us in our Jesus-centered faith. The religion of Christianity seeks the right beliefs of orthodoxy and the right practices of orthopraxy. This is a project that requires the entire church of historic length and ecumenical width—it is not something that can be accomplished by a single individual seeking a private relationship with the divine.

We often hear that "religion doesn't save you." Of course not. That's not what it's intended to do. Jesus Christ is the salvation of God, not Christianity. Jesus Christ is the Savior of the world, not some religion (including the secular religion of progressivism). The Christian religion has a twofold purpose. First, to preserve and pass on the gospel of Jesus Christ. Those of us who have a personal relationship with Jesus can thank the Christian religion for making this possible. Without the Christian religion, Jesus would be almost entirely unknown—certainly less known than his Jewish contemporary Philo of Alexandria. The presence of the Christian religion makes faith in Jesus Christ possible for future generations. Second, the Christian religion intends to form people in Christlikeness—this is the orthopraxy aspect of Christianity. Thus in the Christian religion we train people in prayer by giving them well-crafted prayers because the primary purpose of prayer is not to get God to do what we think God ought to do but to be properly formed.

The following construct is one more way of thinking about the distinction between Christ, the church, and Christianity:

God gave us Jesus. "God so loved the world that he gave his only Son" (Jn 3:16). The salvation of the world doesn't come from the human construct of religion but from God. We cannot save ourselves, but we can cooperate with the salvation of God found in Jesus Christ.

Jesus gave us the church. The church is Jesus' idea, not ours. As Jesus said, "on this rock I will build *my* church" (Mt 16:18). Before casually dismissing the necessity and viability of the church, we should remember whose idea it is.

The church created Christianity. It is the task of the church to establish the proper beliefs and practices that constitute Christianity. But this is an ongoing project subject to alteration. In setting forth how faith in Christ should be practiced by Gentile believers, the Council of Jerusalem around the year AD 50 sent a letter saying, "It has seemed good to the Holy Spirit and to us" (Acts 15:28). The letter then goes on to set forth some orthopraxy guidelines for the Gentile believers, including a prohibition against eating blood and meat sacrificed to idols. This is an example of guidelines that are in flux and may change over time. The prohibition of eating meat sacrificed to idols may have seemed reasonable and workable in Jerusalem, but once Paul got into the Gentile world, he found it was not as simple as James and the Jerusalem elders had imagined. Paul later wrote to the Gentile believers in Corinth saying, "Eat whatever is sold in the meat market without raising any question on the ground of conscience, for 'the earth and its fullness are the Lord's'" (1 Cor 10:25-26).

Here we see early Christianity employing creative theology in order to adapt to a cultural context, and we see it being done within the canon of the New Testament! Very early in the Christian religion, eating blood and meat sacrificed to idols was prohibited, but soon thereafter that position was rethought and modified. There is a remarkable degree of flexibility and capacity for change within the Christian religion. Among other things, this means that we can rethink and even modify Christianity without losing Jesus.

Christianity is an ongoing project to understand God as revealed in Jesus Christ, but Jesus is not a prisoner to Christianity. The one who descended to the dead to lead captivity captive is not a prisoner of anything! Christianity seeks to understand Christ, but Christianity does not create or control Christ. And the radical freedom of Christ is such that he can show up in unexpected places and surprising ways—even among those who are attempting to control him for their own purposes. One of the best examples of this is how Jesus seems to come to life and act on his own in Fyodor Dostoevsky's masterpiece *The Brothers Karamazov*. In the famous chapter "The Grand Inquisitor," everyone seems to lose control of Jesus. It's perhaps the most remarkable passage in this remarkable novel.

THE GRAND INQUISITOR

The Brothers Karamazov is a brilliant theological novel disguised as a patricidal murder mystery. As the title suggests, the novel is primarily centered on the three Karamazov brothers—Dmitri, the impetuous military officer; Ivan, the intellectual atheist; and Alyosha, the young novice monk. It's hard not to suggest that the three brothers represent three aspects of the human experience—the sensual, the intellectual, and the spiritual. (If we include Smerdyakov among the brothers, we can add the demonic.) In one of the most important scenes in the novel, Ivan, the atheistic university student, invites Alyosha, his religious younger brother, to join him in a tavern where Ivan seeks to undermine Alyosha's Christian faith. Ivan begins his assault by raising the problem of evil as seen in the suffering of children and then moves in for the kill by presenting Alyosha with what he calls his poem of "The Grand Inquisitor."

In "The Grand Inquisitor," Jesus appears in the sixteenth century to Seville during the Spanish Inquisition. In his parable, Ivan says, "He appeared quietly, inconspicuously, but, strange to say, everyone recognized him." In Seville, Christ leads a procession of joyful people to the cathedral as they cry, "Hosanna!" They arrive just as a seven-year-old girl in a casket is being carried into the cathedral for her funeral. The grief-stricken mother says, "If it is you, then raise my child!"[2]

> The procession halts, the little coffin is lowered onto the porch at his feet. He looks with compassion and his lips once again softly uttered: *Talitha cumi*—"and the damsel arose." The girl arises in her coffin, sits up and, smiling, looks around in wide-eyed astonishment. She is still holding the bunch of white roses with which she had been lying in the coffin. There is a commotion among the people, cries, weeping, and at this very moment the Cardinal Grand Inquisitor himself crosses the square in front of the cathedral. He is an old man, almost ninety, tall and straight, with a gaunt face and sunken eyes from which a glitter still shines like a fiery spark. . . . He scowls with his thick, gray eyebrows, and his eyes shine with a sinister fire. He stretches forth his finger and orders the guard to take him. And such is his power, so tamed, submissive, and tremblingly obedient to his will are the people, that the crowd immediately parts before the guard, and they, amidst the deathly silence that has suddenly fallen, lay their hands on him and lead him away.[3]

Despite the miracle of raising a little girl from the dead, Christ is arrested by the Grand Inquisitor and imprisoned in a gloomy cell. Late that night, the old man comes to interrogate the prisoner. Though the prisoner never speaks, the Inquisitor, like everyone else, knows who he is. But unlike the laypeople who rejoiced at his coming, the Cardinal Grand Inquisitor is incensed that Christ has appeared in Seville and says, "Why, then, have you come to interfere with us? For you have come to interfere with us and you know it yourself. But do you know what will happen tomorrow? . . . Tomorrow I shall condemn you and burn you at the stake as the most evil of heretics."[4]

In his interrogation of Christ the old Cardinal insists that in his first coming, Christ did everything wrong. The Inquisitor especially accuses Christ of having made the wrong choice in all three wilderness temptations. The Inquisitor says he should have followed the counsel presented by "the powerful and intelligent spirit in the wilderness"—he *should* have turned the stones to bread; he *should* have leaped from the temple; he *should* have bowed down to "the dread spirit" and taken Caesar's sword, for then he would have established a kingdom everyone could recognize and embrace.[5] The Inquisitor insists that he and those like him have spent fifteen centuries correcting Christ's mistake, saying, "Had you accepted the world and Caesar's purple, you would have founded a universal kingdom and granted universal peace. . . . And so we took Caesar's sword, and in taking it, of course, we rejected you and followed *him*."[6] For his interference in the established order of Christendom, the Inquisitor condemns Christ to a second death.

> Tomorrow, I repeat, you will see this obedient flock, which at my first gesture will rush to heap hot coals around your stake, at which I shall burn you for having come to interfere with us. For if anyone has ever deserved our stake, it is you. Tomorrow I shall burn you. *Dixi*.[7]

In his bitter cynicism, Ivan portrays Christianity as nothing but tyranny and bad faith. (Though it is unlikely that Dostoevsky ever read Nietzsche, Ivan seems to embody many of Nietzsche's ideas—especially the idea of Christian love as nothing but "slave morality.") In Ivan's parable, despite the verdict of the Inquisitor, Christ is not burned at the stake. "The Grand Inquisitor" ends like this:

> When the Inquisitor fell silent, he waited for some time for his prisoner to reply. His silence weighed on him. He had seen how the captive listened to him all the while intently

and calmly, looking him straight in the eye, and apparently not wishing to contradict anything. The old man would have liked him to say something, even something bitter, terrible. But suddenly he approaches the old man in silence and gently kisses him on his bloodless, ninety-year-old lips. That is the whole answer. The old man shudders. Something stirs at the corners of his mouth; he walks to the door, opens it, and says to him: "Go and do not come again . . . do not come at all . . . never, never!" And he lets him out into the dark squares of the city. The prisoner goes away.

And the old man?

The kiss burns in his heart, but the old man holds to his former idea.[8]

In the plot of the novel, Ivan's motive in telling the parable of the Grand Inquisitor is to undermine his brother's Christian faith. Ivan is insinuating that the church, or at least its hierarchy, doesn't believe what it claims to believe and that the cardinals and bishops are, in fact, atheists—religious atheists who keep up appearances for the sake of maintaining social order and providing peace of mind for the masses. At one point in his late-night harangue, the Inquisitor says to Christ regarding the millions who believe the teachings of the church, "Peacefully they will die, peacefully they will expire in your name, and beyond the grave they will find only death. But we will keep the secret."[9] This is Ivan's *coup de grâce* intended to finish off Alyosha's faith.

But Ivan's death blow fails to destroy Alyosha's faith. Why? Because of the very thing that makes the parable so compelling—the presence of Christ in the story. "The Grand Inquisitor" is one of the most remarkable pieces of writing in all of Western literature. It has been studied and commented on by thinkers, philosophers, theologians, and literary critics since its appearance in 1880. It's a fiction writer (Dostoevsky) writing about a fictitious writer's piece of fiction. Though "The Grand Inquisitor" takes up twenty pages, Christ is never mentioned by name, and Dostoevsky does not dare to place any words in the mouth of Christ. (The only time Christ speaks in the parable is when he says "*Talitha cumi*" to raise the little girl—a quotation from Mark 5:41.)

The one unique action of Christ in "The Grand Inquisitor" is the kiss—the kiss that still burns in the old man's heart. It seems to me that in this remarkable passage of literature, Ivan Karamazov loses control of Jesus as he appears to come to life within the story and act in a way that surprises the Grand Inquisitor, Ivan, Alyosha, the reader, and maybe even Dostoevsky himself! Christ kisses his would-be executioner. What does the kiss mean? The kiss is not Christ blessing the Grand Inquisitor for his wicked idea; we're told that *despite* the kiss that burns in his heart, "the old man holds to his former idea." The Inquisitor recognizes that Christ's kiss has the potential to change him, but he stubbornly refuses to change.

Christ is not blessing the Grand Inquisitor for his atheism and deceptions, rather Christ is expressing his unconditional love for an old man lost in a prison of his own making. It's not Christ who is a prisoner in the Inquisitor's dungeon; it's the Inquisitor himself. But even now there's hope for the bitter old man and all like him. Jesus Christ is the Logos of God's eternal love in human flesh. So how does Christ—even in a novel—respond to cruel rejection and cynical accusation? With a kiss of eternal love.

And how does Alyosha respond to Ivan's attempt to mock and even poison his faith? This is the best part of the whole re-markable passage. During their long conversation in the tavern (taking up three chapters), Ivan has repeatedly insisted that "without God everything is permitted." He tells his brother that he intends to live according to this formula, an ethic without mo-rality. Ivan plans to "drown in depravity" and at age thirty "return his ticket" by committing suicide. The two brothers have chosen two very different paths. The long conversation in the tavern ends like this:

> Ivan suddenly spoke with unexpected feeling . . . "The formula, 'everything is permitted,' I will not renounce, and what then? Will you renounce me for that? Will you?"
>
> Alyosha stood up, went over to him in silence, and gently kissed him on the lips.[10]

That is the whole answer. Alyosha's response to Ivan is to imitate Christ's response to the Inquisitor—with a kiss of unconditional love. The only reason Christ can kiss the old man in the fiction of "The Grand Inquisitor" is that there really was and is a Christ who loves unconditionally and eternally prays from the cross, "Father, forgive them; for they know not what they do" (Lk 23:34 KJV). Alyosha's inspiration is to imitate Christ—which is what it means to be a Christian.

And what about the Grand Inquisitor? The old man is lost, but not doomed. The kiss still burns in his heart, and therein lies the hope of salvation. All he has to do is turn toward the warmth of unconditional love and he will begin to find his way out of the ice chamber of his self-imposed hell. Dostoevsky introduces this idea later in the novel when Elder Zosima—Dostoevsky's response to Ivan's faith-rejecting argument—says, "I ask myself: 'What is hell? And I answer thus: 'The suffering of being no longer able to love.'"[11] And what is the way out of this hell? To turn to the one who compassionately kisses sinners in their sin and receive his unconditional love. Does Christ damn bitter atheists and angry apostates? No, he kisses them and waits patiently for their hearts to melt.

In *The Brothers Karamazov*, we find Ivan, and maybe even Dostoevsky, losing control of Jesus as he transcends narrative control and acts according to his nature of unconditional love. But what if we fear that we haven't just lost control of Jesus but have lost

Jesus altogether? Take heart, the story is not over. Often when we feel like we have lost Jesus, we are actually in the process of *rediscovering* Jesus.

MARY'S HOME ALONE MOMENT

During the years between his infancy and the beginning of his ministry, we know virtually nothing about the life of Jesus. What happened during those so-called missing years? Contrary to wild speculations of sensationalist books and documentaries, Jesus didn't go to India to study Buddhism or to Alexandria to study Greek philosophy. Jesus lived and worked in Nazareth, quietly plying his trade in construction and faithfully practicing his religion as a devout Jew. Jesus didn't live as an ascetic seeker wandering in foreign lands; he lived in Nazareth as a humble carpenter practicing his religion. We're not told much about the missing thirty years because there's not much to tell. He grew up, learned his trade, worked six days a week, and attended the synagogue on Sabbath. But there is one remarkable story.

As part of a religious community, Jesus' family observed the Sabbath, attended synagogue, and celebrated the Jewish festivals. Every year Joseph and Mary, with their extended family and friends, made the five-day pilgrimage to Jerusalem to celebrate the Passover. It was the biggest and most anticipated event of the year. Jesus had gone to Passover since he was a babe in arms, but when he was twelve, on the verge of being considered an adult, something momentous happened. At some point during the festival, Jesus went to the temple, began asking questions of the scholars, and stayed for three days! The group of pilgrims from Nazareth had already left Jerusalem, and it was a full day before Mary realized that Jesus was not in the caravan. We can imagine the conversation: "Joseph, have you seen Jesus?" Joseph responds, "No, I thought he was with you." It was Mary's *Home Alone* moment. In a panic, Joseph and Mary rushed back to Jerusalem to search for their lost son. It wasn't until the third day that they finally found him in the temple, calmly sitting and discussing Scripture with the scholars. In a roller-coaster of emotion familiar to every parent, Mary went from panic to relief to anger. "When his parents saw him they were astonished; and his mother said to him, 'Child, why have you treated us like this? Look, your father and I have been searching for you in great anxiety'" (Lk 2:48).

I think we all have sympathy for Mary. Twelve-year-old boys aren't permitted to wander off and be absent for three days without telling anyone. But this isn't just any boy, this is the Word in boyhood; this is the Logos in adolescence. It's unsettling that Jesus is so blasé and unapologetic for his actions; if any other boy acted this way, we would consider it insufferable imperiousness. Jesus doesn't say, "I'm sorry, mother. I should have considered how my actions would upset you." What he *does* say are the first recorded words of Christ: "Why were you searching for me? Did you not know that I must be in my Father's house?" (Lk 2:49). These are not easy words to accept or understand—and Mary and Joseph *didn't* understand them. Luke tells us plainly, "But they did not understand what he said to them" (Lk 2:50). And this wouldn't be the last time people found it difficult to understand Jesus' words and actions.

Often the first effect Jesus has on us is disorientation as he constantly forces us to question our assumptions. This strange episode from Jesus' boyhood is a story about losing Jesus. Mary had conceived and given birth to Jesus, she had nursed him and raised him, and she knew him better than anyone. Then she lost Jesus. After a three day agonizing search, she found him again, but he was different. And Mary was forced to reevaluate what she thought she knew about Jesus. Luke ends the story by telling us, "his mother stored all these things in her heart" (Lk 2:51 NLT).

About twenty years later, Mary lost Jesus again. In his early thirties Jesus left Nazareth to hear his cousin John the Baptist preach in Judea. After being baptized, Jesus slipped off into the Judean wilderness for forty days of prayer and fasting. When he finally returned to Galilee, he did not go home to Nazareth and his carpenter's trade but begin preaching the kingdom of God from village to village. What did Jesus' family think of his new vocation? Mark tells us, "When his family heard it, they went out to seize him, for they were saying, 'He is out of his mind'" (Mk 3:21 ESV). Obviously, Jesus' family was not prepared for him to leave the family business and become an itinerate prophet. So they went looking for him. When his family finally found Jesus forty miles away in Capernaum, he was speaking about the kingdom of God in a crowded house.

> Then his mother and brothers came; and standing outside, they sent to him and called him. A crowd was sitting around him; and they said to him, "Your mother and brothers and sisters are outside, asking for you." And he replied, "Who are my mother and my brothers?" And looking at those who sat around him, he said, "Here are my mother and my brothers! Whoever does the will of God is my brother and sister and mother." (Mk 3:31-35)

For a second time, Mary had lost Jesus. And after searching for him, she found him in Capernaum. In Jerusalem, a twelve-year-old Jesus told his mother he had to be in his Father's house. Now in Capernaum, Jesus in young manhood tells his mother that his true family is defined by something other than kinship. Every time Mary lost Jesus, she found him again but had to rethink him. Mary would lose Jesus one more time—again for three days in Jerusalem. Mary would lose Jesus on Good Friday and find him again on

Easter Sunday. After that, she would have to rethink Jesus in the ultimate sense.

Losing Jesus. Finding Jesus. Rethinking Jesus. This is the only way we make spiritual progress. Just about the time we think we've got Jesus figured out, he goes missing. We may fear that we've lost Jesus, nevertheless if we seek him, we will find him. But in the rediscovery we will be required to rethink some things. And that's what repentance means—to rethink things in the light of Christ.

During the many decades that I've sought to live as a follower of Jesus, I've had the experience of losing Jesus several times. It's usually been something like Mary and Joseph's experience of suddenly realizing they couldn't find Jesus in the caravan they assumed he was in. It can be very distressing to realize you can no longer find Jesus in the movement you belong to. I first knew Christ in the Jesus movement and later in the charismatic movement, but there came a day when I could no longer find him there. I could either pretend everything was all right or seek to rediscover Jesus. The seeking may be distressing, but it is the inevitable pattern of spiritual growth. We have Jesus. We lose Jesus. We seek Jesus. We find Jesus. We rethink Jesus. We grow. I don't think it can be otherwise. Craig Barnes says,

> The deep fear behind every loss is that we have been abandoned by the God who should have saved us. The transforming moment in Christian conversion comes when we realize that even God has left us. We then discover it was not God, but our image of God that abandoned us. This frees us to discover more of the mystery of God than we knew. Only then is change possible.[12]

Idols don't move. You can always find them where you left them. But the living God will occasionally abscond from familiar confines. We can never retire from being a seeker. So if it feels like you've lost Jesus, don't give up; keep searching. Seek for him in the places where Mary found him. Look for him in the temple—the new temple made of living stones. Look for him in the houses where people gather to hear about the kingdom of God. Look for him in new movements if you have to. There are plenty of other people who have gone through a similar experience of losing Jesus for a season. Sometimes we need to let the faith of others carry us. If our faith is paralyzed, we can be like the man lowered through the roof into the presence of Jesus by his friends. When you can't depend on your own faith, trust the faith of your friends (see Lk 5:17-26). Look for Jesus in the Gospels. Don't try to feel Jesus or figure him out, just watch what he does and listen to what he says in the Gospel stories. I'm acquainted with a well-known Christian leader who during a spiritual crisis could read nothing from the Bible other than the Gospels. That was a healthy instinct, and eventually she was able to rediscover Jesus in a new way.

The sense of being abandoned by God, losing Jesus, is all part of the long spiritual journey. The sixteenth-century Spanish mystic John of the Cross described it as the dark night of the soul. These are the trying times when God plays a mischievous game of hide-and-seek. But it's all designed to draw us out of our cozy spirituality and onto the hard road of an earnest quest. Christ is found by those who seek him, not those who presume him. Being disturbed into action by the apparent absence of Jesus is far better than slipping away into the spiritual malaise of being nothing more than comfortably numb.

> Ask, and it will be given to you; seek, and you will find; knock, and it will be opened to you. For everyone who asks receives, and the one who seeks finds, and to the one who knocks it will be opened. (Mt 7:7-8)

6

THE DARK NIGHT
OF UNKNOWING

God called the light Day, and the darkness he called Night.
And there was evening and there was morning, one day.

GENESIS 1:5 RSV

I n Genesis, the new day doesn't begin at sunrise or at midnight, but at sunset. Reflecting this, the Jewish Sabbath does not begin at sunrise on Saturday but at sundown on Friday. Each new day begins with new darkness. Newness is not heralded by the rising sun but by enfolding darkness. This is counterintuitive. The new day does not begin with being able to see, the new day begins with being *unable* to see. Newness is born in nothingness. God creates *ex nihilo*. Darkness is the canvass for the new light of creation.

And in our pilgrimage through life, dark nights come before new dawns. This is good news for a troubled soul groping in

Stygian darkness. A dark night of the soul does not have to be the end of a faith journey but can be the beginning of a new journey that leads deeper into the mystery of God. Often our spiritual progress does not begin with a day of new knowing, as we tend to think, but with a dark night of unknowing. Holding on to certitude in a dogged insistence that we already have the answers prevents progress. Spiritual progress is not attained by a formula of knowing plus knowing plus knowing. Despite what we may assume, spiritual growth is not the result of endless addition. Spiritual growth also requires subtraction. Spiritual progress is not knowing, knowing, knowing; spiritual progress is more often knowing, *un*knowing, *new* knowing. The sun doesn't unceasingly rise, the sun also sets. In our long journey into the mystery of God, progress is usually experienced like this: daytime . . . dark night . . . new dawn.

One of the primary archetypes of spiritual development in Scripture is the story of Abraham—the father of faith. Abraham is a man defined by faith because he was willing to venture into the unknown. When Abraham was called by God to go on a journey, the writer of Hebrews tells us, "he set out, not knowing where he was going" (Heb 11:8). Abraham's journey of faith began as a journey into the dark night of unknowing. The living God was leading Abraham into something all new because it was entirely unknown. Abraham's journey from Ur to Canaan is a pivotal episode in the salvation story told in the Bible. It also represents an entirely new movement in the Genesis story. Until Abraham, all the journeys in Genesis are eastward and away from God.

> [God] drove out the man, and at the *east* of the garden of Eden
> he placed the cherubim and a flaming sword that turned
> every way to guard the way to the tree of life. (Gen 3:24 ESV)

Then Cain went away from the presence of the Lord, and settled in the land of Nod, *east* of Eden. (Gen 4:16)

It came about as they journeyed *east*, that they found a plain in the land of Shinar and settled there. (Gen 11:2 NASB)

Whether it's Adam banished from Eden or Cain fleeing the divine presence or the postdiluvian world seeking a place to build the tower of Babel, the migration is always east and always away from God. As the story is told in Genesis, the world east of Eden—the land of Nod and the plains of Shinar—is the world of idolatry. But then God intervenes by calling an idolater from the Babylonian city of Ur to leave the old gods and move to a new life in a new land. When Abraham responds by faith to God's call and journeys to the land of Canaan, it is a migration in a new direction—westward. *Go west, old man.* But a journey into the west is a journey into the land of the setting sun—it's a journey toward darkness. This is the counterintuitive pattern of Genesis. A journey into new light is first a journey into the dark night of unknowing. Of course, we instinctively fear the darkness, so we may balk at such a journey.

We may prefer to stay where we are, stay with what we know, and pretend that we are content. Complacency, not doubt, is the great enemy of spiritual development. Abraham becomes the father of faith because he was willing to be led beyond the comfortable confines of idolatrous Ur, where God is deeply misunderstood. Ur is not our true home; Ur is just where we were born. Home is a place far from where we were born. The story of salvation in our life is the story of finding our way home to the Father's house of love.

In George MacDonald's fantasy novel *Lilith*, the central character, Mr. Vane, encounters the mysterious Mr. Raven—a spiritual guide who sometimes appears as a raven and at other times as an old librarian. Mr. Raven comes to Mr. Vane to lead him on a soul-saving journey into another world, but Mr. Vane is hesitant to embark on such a strange journey. The second time Mr. Raven comes to visit Mr. Vane at his home, their conversation goes like this:

> "Now we should be going!" said the raven, and stepped to the front porch.
>
> "Going where?" I asked.
>
> "Going where we have to go," he answered. "You did not surely think you had got home? I told you there was no going out and in at pleasure until you were at home!"
>
> "I do not want to go," I said.
>
> "That does not make any difference—at least not much," he answered. "This is the way!"
>
> "I am quite content where I am."
>
> "You think so, but you are not. Come along."[1]

The wise Mr. Raven knows that Mr. Vane's true home was a place where he'd not yet been. We think we are content in our settled certitude because we don't know what we don't know. Our ignorance is bliss. Our satisfaction is sedation. We're content with life in Ur, filled with idols and wrong ideas about God, because we've never been anywhere else or known anything else. So God in his mercy sends us a Mr. Raven—a guide to help us find our way home, a place yet unknown. We all have to go on a spiritual journey because we're all born a long way from home. At times, the journey home leads us through dark places, but that doesn't mean we are lost.

> Sometimes the best map will not guide you
> You can't see what's round the bend
> Sometimes the road leads through dark places
> Sometimes the darkness is your friend[2]

Going through the dark night of unknowing (which some call deconstruction) doesn't mean you've gone wrong or gotten lost, even though it may feel like it. We think certitude is right because it feels right, but it's wrong—it's a false sense of security that lulls us into spiritual lethargy. This is why God sends us a Mr. Raven to tell us, "You think you are content, but you are not. Come along." Like Mr. Raven in *Lilith*, our raven can come to us in different forms—a friend, a book, a nagging question, a growing unease, a tragedy, a season of deep suffering. At last we begin to move and we find ourselves on the road away from the home that never was home, and seeking a home where we've never been. Inevitably, the road at times passes through dark places, and we begin to doubt if we'll ever make it home. Disturbing thoughts rise unbidden; thoughts like, *I'm not so sure anymore. I'm not confident at all. I don't know what I'm doing. I don't know where I'm going. I don't know where this is all headed.* These are normal thoughts that can arise in a soul that is making genuine spiritual progress through spiritual darkness. "And there was evening and there was morning, one day." The new day of new knowing is preceded by the dark night of unknowing.

Unknowing can have two meanings—*not* knowing and *un*-knowing. There are things we don't know and need to learn. And there are things we think we know and need to relearn. Abraham's journey of unknowing was mostly about not knowing. "By faith Abraham . . . set out, not knowing where he was going" (Heb 11:8). But there is a journey of unknowing that is mostly about *un*-knowing or unlearning. It's not the learning that is hard but the unlearning. In the first half of life, we tend to think that all we need for spiritual progress is positive addition. Just learn some more God stuff. But in the second half of life, spiritual progress is more often obtained through the apophatic process of negation. We begin to know about God by realizing how very little we know about God. If Abraham's dark night of unknowing was about *not* knowing, Paul's dark night of unknowing was about *un*-knowing.

BLINDED BY THE LIGHT

Saul of Tarsus was a biblical scholar, a devout Pharisee, and, as most Pharisees are, a zealous practitioner of religious certitude. His zeal was exhibited in his relentless persecution of the Way—a new Jewish sect proclaiming that Jesus of Nazareth, a crucified Galilean, was Israel's Messiah. Saul dedicated his formidable skills of scholarship and debate to opposing this sect. Saul *knew* that Jesus of Nazareth could not be the Messiah because the Bible said so. Saul could prove it by citing chapter and verse. Deuteronomy 21:23 says, "Anyone hung on a tree is under God's curse." Jesus of Nazareth was hung on a tree, therefore he was under God's curse: therefore he cannot be the Messiah. Point proved. End of the debate. Saul was certain that the Bible *proved* Jesus was not the Messiah. It was clear as day. And something had to be done about the heretics who claimed that Jesus was the Messiah.

Years later, Saul—now known as the apostle Paul—explained to King Agrippa his violent zeal against the Christians like this:

> Indeed, I myself was convinced that I ought to do many things against the name of Jesus of Nazareth. And that is what I did in Jerusalem; with authority received from the chief priests, I not only locked up many of the saints in prison, but I also cast my vote against them when they were being condemned to death. By punishing them often in all the synagogues I tried to force them to blaspheme; and since I was so furiously enraged at them, I pursued them even to foreign cities. (Acts 26:9-11)

Saul was furiously enraged because he was certain that he was right and the Christians were wrong. Biblical certainty was the drug of choice for this young Pharisee, but it only made him mean. Certitude can be an incubator for cruelty. Perceived infallibility can lead to brutality.

Aleksandr Solzhenitsyn was one of the most important Christian writers of the twentieth century, but before his conversion, he was a convinced atheist and zealous communist. In *The Gulag Archipelago*, Solzhenitsyn writes of his youthful arrogance and how conversion came to him as a prisoner in a Soviet gulag:

> In the intoxication of youthful success I had felt myself to be infallible, and I was therefore cruel. In my most evil moments I was convinced that I was doing good, and I was well supplied with systematic arguments. It was only when I lay on rotting prison straw that I sensed within myself the first stirrings of good. Gradually it was disclosed to me that the line separating good and evil passes not through states, nor between classes, nor between political parties—but right through every human heart and through all human hearts. This line shifts. Inside us, it oscillates with the years. It is impossible to expel evil from the world in its entirety, but it is possible to constrict it within each person. And that is why I turn back to the years of my imprisonment and say, sometimes to the astonishment of those about me: "*Bless you, prison!*" I nourished my soul there, and I say it without hesitation: "*Bless you, prison*, for having been in my life."[3]

In their youth, Saul of Tarsus and Aleksandr Solzhenitsyn were similar—they both felt they were infallible and therefore were cruel. Certitude manifested itself in sheer meanness. Saul ransacked synagogues in search of heretics. He rounded up members of the Way and imprisoned them. He presided over the stoning of Stephen, the first Christian martyr. When Saul had done his worst in Jerusalem, he obtained authorization from the chief priests to search for heretics in the synagogues of Damascus. Armed with arrest warrants and harboring threats of murder, Saul marched with a mean stride to Damascus.

It's at least a week's worth of walking from Jerusalem to Damascus. And though Caravaggio's famous painting depicts Saul with a horse, he probably walked. I've been on some extended pilgrimages and here's what I know about long walks—it gives you time to think. And if Saul was anything, he was a thinker. Saul stormed out of Jerusalem and headed for Damascus "breathing threats and murder" (Acts 9:1). But a long walk has a way of drawing you into a more contemplative state. What was Saul thinking? He was thinking about Jesus of Nazareth and the preposterous claim by some that this crucified Galilean was the risen Messiah. He was thinking how he *knew* that couldn't be true because Deuteronomy says a crucified man is cursed by God. But . . .

Did other thoughts begin to interfere with Saul's certitude? Of course, we can't really know, but we do know that Saul had a thorough grasp of the biblical text. Did he begin to wonder about Psalm 22 where David says, "they pierced my hands and my feet" (Ps 22:16 KJV)? Did Saul think, *David's hands and feet were never pierced—who is he talking about?* Did Saul muse on what Isaiah meant when he says of the messianic Servant,

> We accounted him stricken,
>   struck down by God, and afflicted.
> But he was wounded for our transgressions,
>   crushed for our iniquities. (Is 53:4-5)

We don't know, but it's hard for me to believe that during his long walk, some of these thoughts didn't arise in the mind of a Scripture scholar like Saul. The combustible material for a spiritual explosion was already present in Saul's mind, and it would only take a spark to ignite it. We don't know exactly what Saul was thinking as he neared Damascus, but we do know that as he came to the end of his long walk, there was a flash of light, Saul fell to the ground and heard a voice saying, "Saul, Saul, why do you persecute me?" An astonished Saul responded, "Who are you, Lord?" (Acts 9:4-5).

When Saul asked the Voice coming from the light "Who are you, Lord?" he is not asking, "Who are you, *sir*?" but who are you, *Lord*?" Lord (*kyrios*) was the word a pious Greek-speaking Jew used to refer to the eternal "I am" who dwells in unapproachable light and whose name is unmentionable. Saul knows that the one speaking to him from a light brighter than the sun must be the same one Ezekiel encountered when he said, "The heavens were opened and I saw visions of God. . . . [S]eated above the likeness of a throne was something that seemed like a human form. . . . When I saw it, I fell on my face, and I heard the voice of someone speaking" (Ezek 1:1, 26, 28).

The divine manifestation that Ezekiel encountered by the River Chebar is the same Saul encountered on the Damascus Road. Saul knows that like Ezekiel, he is experiencing a vision of the Lord God but dares to ask, "Who *are* you?" The answer from the light not only changed Saul's life but would also ultimately change the world: "I am Jesus, whom you are persecuting" (Acts 9:5). How can we begin to fathom the impact that must have had on a supremely self-confident Pharisee like Saul of Tarsus? In *Paul: A Biography*, N. T. Wright imagines Saul on the Damascus Road seeing the same glorious figure seen by Ezekiel five centuries earlier:

> Saul of Tarsus, head full of scripture, heart full of zeal, raises his eyes slowly upward once more. He is seeing now, eyes wide open, conscious of being wide awake but conscious also that there seems to be a rift in reality, a fissure in the fabric of the cosmos, and that his waking eyes are seeing things so dangerous that if he were not so prepared, so purified, so carefully devout, he would never have dared

to come this far. Upward again, from the chest to the face. He raises his eyes to see the one he has worshipped and served all his life . . . And he comes face to face with Jesus of Nazareth.[4]

Saul had seen the Light and had gone blind. Luke tells us, "Saul got up from the ground, and though his eyes were open, he could see nothing; so they led him by the hand and brought him into Damascus" (Acts 9:8). Saul saw the truth in the blinding flash of light and was thrust into total darkness. Saul had gone from the high noon of certitude into the dark night of unknowing. Saul could no longer strut with a mean and menacing stride; he could only shuffle in the faltering steps of a man suddenly struck blind. Instead of marching down the road with arrogant confidence, Saul gropes his way through the darkness needing someone to lead him by the hand. At last Saul was making progress.

In a blinding moment of divine revelation, Saul knew that Jesus was Lord—and he knew nothing else. Saul had entered his nocturnal negation, his dark night of unknowing. Saul had been Jerusalem's Bible Answer Man—he knew his Bible and had all the answers. But now he didn't know anything except that the one he had met as God on the Damascus Road was Jesus. The cognitive dissonance induced by this truth was extreme to the utmost. "For three days he was without sight, and neither ate nor drank" (Acts 9:9). Saul was not so much fasting as he was too stunned to eat or drink.

Everything he had thought he knew he now had to rethink in the light of the one solitary truth he had: Jesus is God. Saul's theological world had been suddenly and totally deconstructed. His confidently constructed certitude has been vaporized the moment the Voice spoke from the blinding light saying, "I am Jesus." Now Saul sees nothing. He's blind. He knows nothing. Nothing makes sense. This is not Saul's conversion but his devastating deconstruction. His radical delearning. Saul's theological house has not been remodeled but has been razed to the ground. So what does Saul do during his three days of utter darkness? Luke tells us he prayed. What does he pray? I'm sure he prayed the Shema—the essential prayer of the Jewish people.

Sh'ma Yisrael Adonai Eloheinu Adonai Echad.

Hear, O Israel: The LORD is our God, the LORD alone. You shall love the LORD your God with all your heart, and with all your soul, and with all your might. (Deut 6:4-5)

In his dark night of unknowing, Saul is deconstructing all the way down to the one great commandment of the Shema. Saul no longer knows everything. All he knows now is that Jesus has been revealed to him as the one God. And he knows that he is to love the one God with all his heart. But in the blinding light of Christ that has led him into absolute darkness, he has to rethink everything. *Hear, O Israel.* But what does it mean to be Israel? *The LORD is our God.* But what does it mean that Jesus of Nazareth is the God of Israel? *You shall love the LORD your God.* But how? His zealous love for God brought him to Damascus with hate in his heart and the intention to visit violence upon the church there. Yes, Saul now had to rethink everything. Of course, as a Torah scholar, Saul knew the other great commandment: "You shall love your neighbor as yourself" (Lev 19:18).

While Saul is undergoing his dark night of deconstruction, reduced to praying the first prayer he learned as a child, there is a knock at the door. It was Ananias—one of the Jewish Christians in Damascus. Jesus had appeared to Ananias in a vision and instructed him to find Saul, lay hands on him, heal him, and baptize him.

So Ananias went and entered the house. He laid his hands on Saul and said, "Brother Saul, the Lord Jesus, who appeared to you on your way here, has sent me so that you may regain your sight and be filled with the Holy Spirit." And immediately something like scales fell from his eyes, and his sight was restored. Then he got up and was baptized. (Acts 9:17-18)

It's only as the scales fell from his eyes that Saul experienced his full conversion; it's only after the scales fell from his eyes that Saul is baptized. When did the scales fall from his eyes? When Ananias addresses him as "Brother Saul." At that moment, it all clicks. Jesus is the revelation of God—a God of love. And to love God with all your heart is to love your neighbor as yourself. It all clicks when Ananias calls Saul—who had come to Damascus to harm people like Ananias—"brother." Saul had thought that he could prove his loyalty to God by his violent zeal, but now he understands that loyalty to God can only be proved by love. Much later the apostle Paul will pen the great ode to love that we know as 1 Corinthians 13, but it was in Damascus that he first saw the supremacy of love as the scales fell from his eyes. Paul had thought that he knew everything. Then he suddenly knew he knew nothing. And now he has begun to know that greatest truth of all: God is love. The dark night of unknowing has led to the dawn of knowing everything anew in the light of Christ.

Paul had entered a new day and was well on his way to understanding that love is greater than knowledge, greater than doctrine, greater than zeal, greater than everything. Paul had once been so proud of his knowledge, his doctrine, his zeal, but all of that has changed now. If we think doctrine is more important than love, we already have bad doctrine. Eventually, Paul would write, "And now faith, hope, and love abide, these three; and the greatest of these is love" (1 Cor 13:13). Paul's conversion wasn't from Judaism to Christianity—Paul wouldn't have seen it like that. Paul's conversion was from the zeal of religious violence to the loyalty of cosuffering love. Paul was converted from violence to nonviolence.

One of the things Jesus said about Paul at the time of his conversion was, "I myself will show him how much he must suffer for the sake of my name" (Acts 9:16). Paul would endure suffering for the sake of his God, but he would never again inflict suffering in the name of his God. Paul had come to Damascus to violently persecute Ananias in the name of God. But now he sits at table with Ananias sharing the first meal of his new life. It is a love feast. The scales have indeed fallen from his eyes. If anyone can understand the depth of John Newton's immortal hymn, it's the apostle Paul.

> Amazing grace! How sweet the sound
> That saved a wretch like me.
> I once was lost, but now am found,
> Was blind, but now I see.

On the Damascus Road, Paul experienced a devastating deconstruction of faith. At the table with Ananias, Paul experienced a beautiful reconstruction of faith. A dark night led to a new dawn. For the rest of his life, Paul will live in the light of the single all-encompassing revelation that Jesus Christ is the image of the invisible God. This and this alone is the only possible foundation for Christian faith.

7

THE ONLY FOUNDATION

Without rival, the most important theologian in the history of Christianity is the apostle Paul. The influence of this indefatigable missionary on the formation of Christianity and subsequently the course of Western history is incalculable. More than any other single individual, Paul opened the way for the Western world to turn from its tired paganism and embrace the new faith proclaimed in the gospel of Jesus Christ. But what was the foundation for Paul's world-changing gospel? He tells us in a letter he wrote to the churches in Galatia: "I want you to know, brothers and sisters, that the gospel that was proclaimed by me is not of human origin; for I did not receive it from a human source, nor was I taught it, but I received it through a *revelation* of Jesus Christ" (Gal 1:11-12, emphasis added).

Everything the apostle Paul believed, preached, wrote, and did was built on the foundation of the *revelation* of Jesus Christ given to him by God. Paul did not come to the knowledge that Jesus is the Lord God of Israel by a series of deductions or through a careful process of logic. Paul's gospel is built entirely on revelation—a divine disclosure independent of human reason. Paul didn't read the Bible and finally figure out that Jesus is the Messiah as if he were a theological Sherlock Holmes sleuthing out the evidence. No! God *revealed* this to Paul. And as a result of this revelation, he now had to read the Bible in a completely new way. Once we have the revelation that Jesus is the Christ, *then* we can see it in the Old Testament. But we can't start with the Old Testament and reason our way to a logical conclusion that Jesus is the Christ. The light of revelation emanating from Jesus Christ himself illuminates all of Scripture.

Paul insists that apart from the revelation of Christ, the reading of Scripture is obscured by a veil, saying, "only in Christ is it taken away" (2 Cor 3:14 NIV). Revelation is not the end; it's the beginning. Revelation is not the capstone, it's the cornerstone. Revelation is not where we arrive, it's where we begin. Jesus Christ *is* the revelation of God, but this cannot be known independent of God's action upon us. God must take the initiative in revelation, and this is the work of the Holy Spirit. The revelation of Jesus Christ is the *only* possible foundation for Christian faith. Paul is very explicit in stating that his vast knowledge of the Scriptures and his formal training in scriptural interpretation was not how he came to know Jesus as the Christ. Rather he says it occurred when God "was pleased to *reveal* his Son to me" (Gal 1:15-16, emphasis added).

Paul loves the word *revelation*—it's central to his theology. He uses revelation (*apokalypsis*, "to unveil") some thirty times in his letters. And throughout his Epistles, Paul insists that the revelation of Jesus Christ is the only foundation that our faith can securely rest on. As he told the Corinthians, "No other foundation can anyone lay than that which is laid, which is Jesus Christ" (1 Cor 3:11 NKJV). The foundation of Jesus Christ does not rest on *some other* foundation—like the Bible or science or reason. No,

Jesus Christ himself is the bedrock foundation. The apostle Paul knows that the revelation of Jesus Christ is the only reliable basis for our faith. And the apostle Peter knows this too.

When Jesus asked his disciples, "Who do people say that I am?" (Mk 8:27), the disciples related the various theories that were possible explanations for the actions and identity of Jesus of Nazareth: John the Baptist, Elijah, Jeremiah, or one of the prophets. These are the theological conclusions that could be drawn from a particular way of reading the Bible in the first century. But then Jesus asked the all-important question:

> "But who do *you* say that I am?" Simon Peter answered and said, "You are the Christ, the Son of the living God." Jesus answered and said to him, "Blessed are you, Simon Bar-Jonah, for flesh and blood has not *revealed* this to you, but my Father who is in heaven. And I say that you are Peter, and on this rock I will build my church, and the gates of hell shall not prevail against it." (Mt 16:15-18 ESV, emphasis added)

Peter, like Paul, did not figure out who Jesus was through a process of study or a method of logic but through a divine revelation given to him directly by the Father. This revelation changed Simon's identity and he is given a new name. Indeed, the revelation of Jesus Christ is so monumental that it gives every recipient of it a new identity. Jesus tells Simon that henceforth he will call him Peter (*Petros* or Rocky). Jesus then announces that on this bedrock (*petra*) of revelation he will build his church and that nothing—not even the powers of death—will prevail against it. What is the unassailable foundation Christian faith is built on? The God-given revelation of Jesus Christ. The foundation the church is built on is *not* the Bible or theology or reason or historical evidence or apologetics, but the divinely given revelation that Jesus Christ is the Son of God.

Direct knowledge concerning ultimate transcendence is possible only if the transcendent One initiates contact. This God-initiated contact is what Paul means by *revelation*. Christianity is not a series of proofs; it is the confession based on the revelation that Jesus Christ is Lord. Though I claim that Christianity is credible, it is not provable. The revelation of Jesus Christ cannot be proven (or disproven), it can only be proclaimed. And the proclamation can either be believed or disbelieved. But Paul insists that the capacity to believe is inherently present in the proclamation—the proclamation is self-authenticating because it is the word of Christ. "Faith comes from hearing, and hearing by the word of Christ" (Rom 10:17 NASB). The capacity to believe is ontologically present in the proclamation of the gospel.

The writers of the New Testament, who inform all Christian theology, operate from this foundational revelation: Jesus Christ is God among us. They don't *arrive* at that revelation; they *begin* from that revelation. And from that revelation, they returned to their Scriptures (the Hebrew Bible) and interpreted them in a new and distinctively Christian way. For the New Testament writers, "Son of God" is not hyperbole for what a great man Jesus was but the bedrock of their faith. Their Christology was the unabashed claim that Jesus of Nazareth was the God of Israel made human flesh. They have no intention of offering their readers the option for any other conclusion. Karl Barth, the great Swiss theologian who wrote about the supremacy of divine revelation more expansively and more cogently than any other theologian, says it like this:

> Those who thought it [Christology] out and expressed it did not intend to say: We have met a hero or sage or saint, for the adequate description of whom we, in our highest rapture, are left with only provisional terms such as the word of God or God's Son. But here, too, preceding all experiences and possible raptures, knowledge of the divinity of Jesus Christ was

the beginning of the way. Even if the New Testament witnesses also find in Jesus heroic or saintly traits, or the characteristics of a sage, yet that does not mean that we can go on
to say that this was the line along which is to be sought the
distinctive and original thing to be found in Jesus and to be
said about Him. On the contrary all that—so far as traces of it
are to be found in the New Testament—is nothing but the
stammering, inadequate expression of their initial and basic
awareness: we have met God, we have heard His Word—that
is the original and ultimate fact.[1]

Our awareness that in Jesus Christ we have met God is what
Barth calls "the original and ultimate fact." It is the origin and foundational *fact* of our faith. What some may think is the conclusion
is, in reality, the beginning—the only possible beginning. The
knowledge that Jesus is God comes to us by witness and is apprehended by revelation. It cannot be otherwise. If we have any other
beginning point than revelation, Jesus will no longer be the foundation. If we start anywhere other than with the revelation of
Jesus—religion, science, the Bible, theology, philosophy—*that* becomes the foundation. But, as Paul would say, God forbid! There
can be numerous *witnesses* to this revelation, but revelation alone
is the foundation. If we try to make anything else the foundation
for faith, we build on a foundation that ultimately cannot support
the weight of the claim it makes. Deeply informed by Karl Barth,
New Testament scholar Douglas Campbell explains:

> If Christians think that they can prove the existence of God
> acting in Jesus independently of God's revelation of Godself,
> using some higher truth or argument or position that ev-
> eryone acknowledges, they pay a heavy price. These attempts
> might be convincing to the faithful, but they tend to collapse
> under the withering scrutiny of modern philosophers. And a

culture that has been told loudly that God can be proved then feels justified in turning decisively away from God. The only thing that seems to have been proved is that God does not exist. God is rejected as an unproved hypothesis without anyone confronting the place where God has in fact chosen to become known, which is personally, in Jesus.[2]

Barth and Campbell both insist that we must recognize that revelation is the only possible and only reliable foundation for Christian faith. We already know this because it is how we experience the reality of Christ. But modernity has told us that our own experience is invalid because it cannot be empirically verified. If we capitulate to the arrogant and unfounded assertion of modernity that only that which is verifiable in a laboratory is credible, we have agreed to play a rigged game where the very foundation is yanked out from beneath our feet. But if we are embarrassed to claim we believe something that cannot be proven according to the criteria of empiricism's rigged game, the consequences can be catastrophic for our Christian faith.

Historic Christianity is built on the self-authenticating revelation of Jesus Christ and can be neither proved nor disproved by a philosophical method. Modern fundamentalism, on the other hand, built on the shoddy foundation of biblicism, is easily dismantled. Fundamentalism is filled with trapdoors that drop into the abyss of atheism!

Not long ago, I had a conversation with an erstwhile Christian who had recently become an atheist—again, after listening to one of the ubiquitous post-Christian podcasts that tend to confuse modern fundamentalism with historic Christianity. In the course of our conversation, this thoughtful woman readily admitted that she still held a deep admiration for Jesus, but then asked, "Why does Jesus have to be God?" For her, the claim that Jesus is God is a *conclusion* one may or may not reach in considering Jesus. But for the writers of the New Testament, the revelation that Jesus is the Son of God is the *beginning point* of everything. In response to her question, I asked my own question, "What Jesus are we talking about?"

She said, "*You know . . . Jesus.*"

No, I don't know. Tell me, what Jesus are we talking about?

Well, Jesus of Nazareth. The Jesus who preached in Galilee. The Jesus who was crucified by the Romans. Why does that Jesus have to be God?

How do you know that Jesus of Nazareth preached in Galilee and was crucified by the Romans? What is your source for this knowledge?

I guess because it's in the Gospels.

All right then. You believe that Jesus preached in Galilee and was crucified by the Romans because Matthew, Mark, Luke, and John tell you this, but you don't believe this Jesus is God.

That's right.

Did Matthew, Mark, Luke, and John know that Jesus wasn't God and deliberately perpetrated a hoax?

No, they believed Jesus was God.

So they were just, what, stupid?

I wouldn't say they were stupid, they just weren't, I don't know . . .

Modern?

I guess that's it.

So Matthew, Mark, Luke, and John (or whoever the authors of the Gospels were) wrote from a conviction that Jesus of Nazareth was the Son of God, but two thousand years later, you *know* this isn't possible because you're a modern person who listens to podcasts?

My last question may have been a bit snarky, but I did want to point out the inherent arrogance in certain modes of modern thought. Whatever else we may say about empiricist modernity, it's certainly not very humble. The arrogance of modernity is rooted in its uncritical certitude—it is convinced that *all that can be known* can only be known by its method. (Postmodernism may be no friend to Christianity, but it has done us a service in puncturing the puffed-up pride of modernity.)

Modern empiricism begins with the assumption that revelation is impossible and that there are no avenues of knowledge or objects of knowledge that lie outside the scope of empirical inquiry. Obviously, this is a system that has default atheism built into it from the beginning! When a person says, "I refuse to believe in the existence of invisible realities unless I *see* them," they have, by definition, ended the game before it begins. If from the outset you insist that if God doesn't show up in the telescope like Alpha Centauri or in the microscope like a DNA molecule, then God doesn't exist, well, guess what, you're going to "prove" that God doesn't exist. Arguing that the self-sustaining Creator God doesn't exist because God doesn't appear in the category of contingent phenomenon is not a good-faith argument; it's a trick. If you begin with the empiricist assumption, atheism is a foregone conclusion. It's a rigged game. But historic Christianity (as opposed to modern fundamentalism) has always refused to play that game. Historic Christianity refuses to be cowed into accepting modernity's arrogant and unsubstantiated claim that divine revelation is impossible. As Hamlet's ghost said to the rational Horatio, "There are more things in Heaven and Earth, Horatio, / Than are dreamt of in your philosophy."[3]

THE BIBLE IS NOT THE FOUNDATION
OF CHRISTIAN FAITH

Very often Protestant Christians (especially evangelicals) are taught that the foundation for Christian faith is the Bible. This is nearly a universal truism in the evangelical world, evidenced by how most evangelical statements of faith begin with the Bible. Subsequently, if the Bible is the foundation for Christian faith, then the Bible must be defended at all costs—and it tends to be an inerrant, literalist reading of the Bible that must be defended. In this system, a flaw in the Bible is a crack in the foundation that can lead to a catastrophic collapse. This is the anxiety that fuels the sham apologetics of the Ken Ham variety.[4] Betting on the literal scientific and historical accuracy of the Bible is a gamble for the highest stakes. But do we have to bet our faith on Noah's Ark perched atop Mount Ararat or Egyptian chariots rusting beneath the Red Sea? No, it's a fool's errand.

At this point, someone will usually accuse me of having a low view of Scripture. But these accusers are wrong. I don't have a low view of Scripture; I have a high view of Christ. I hold the Scriptures as authoritative in informing and shaping the Christian faith. (Note the hundreds of Scripture references in all my books!) I faithfully affirm the Bible as authoritative in the Christian faith, but the Bible is not where we begin—the Bible is not self-authenticating.

Here's how it works: first, I believe in Jesus—I believe that Jesus is the Christ, the Son of the living God. I believe this because it was first revealed to me when I was fifteen years old. This claim can neither be proven nor disproven; it can only be attested and believed or disbelieved. I didn't study my way to the knowledge that Jesus is God; it was revealed to me. Forty five years of subsequent study of the Bible is the result of the initial revelation of Jesus Christ. I'm seeking to understand what has already been revealed. This is what is meant by Anselm's motto "faith seeking understanding."[5] But this all-important revelation of Jesus Christ was not unmediated. It was made possible by the faithful witness of the church carried down through the centuries. Thus I have come to have a deep and abiding respect for the witness of the church. Then the church says, "Hey BZ, we have a canonical text that we regard as authoritative. It's called the Bible." This is how I come to accept the Bible as authoritative, but it's a three-step process: First Jesus, then church, and finally Bible. To begin with the Bible and make *that* the foundation of faith (instead of Jesus!) is to put more weight on the Bible than the Bible can bear. Let me give just one example.

Christians who have founded their faith on the Bible often face the moral conundrum of slavery. The fact is, in neither Testament does the Bible give a clear denunciation of slavery. The Bible simply takes for granted the institution of slavery and doesn't present any clearly identifiable vision for its abolition. (Though I do insist that in some of Paul's Epistles, we find the *trajectory* for a theology of abolition.) Recently I was speaking to a group of teens at a youth camp in Colorado. My assigned topic was "What's the Deal with the Bible?" I opened my talk with this text from Exodus 21:

> When a slaveowner strikes a male or female slave with a rod
> and the slave dies immediately, the owner shall be punished.
> But if the slave survives a day or two, there is no punishment;
> for the slave is the owner's property. (Ex 21:20-21)

I then made it painfully clear to my young audience what this bronze-age scriptural text says: A Hebrew slaveowner was permitted to beat his slave into unconsciousness; if the slave died a day or two later as a result of the beating, the slaveowner was immune from punishment *because* "the slave is the owner's property." I then asked the teens how many of them disagreed with this scriptural law. I waited until all of them had their hand raised.

I pointed out that they were contradicting the Bible and apparently claiming to have a moral vision superior to the Bible regarding the subject of slavery. They nervously agreed. I then congratulated them, saying, "Of course, you have a superior moral vision regarding the subject of slavery than what is found in Exodus, as you should because you believe in Jesus!" Was I trying to undermine the value of the Bible in the lives of these young Christians? No! I was trying to give them a way to hold on to the Bible for a lifetime. I was trying to head off the possibility of them later in life saying something like, "The Bible supports slavery! I'm done with the Bible and Christianity!" To conflate the Bible and Christian faith into the same thing is a dangerous gambit.

I gave this talk in the Rocky Mountains in an outdoor chapel beneath a grove of tall pine trees. In a moment of inspiration, I gave the teens this illustration: Christian faith is a living tree rooted in Christ and nourished by the soil of Scripture. You cannot remove the tree from the soil and expect it to survive, but neither are we to think that the tree and the soil are the same thing! The Bible and Christianity are not synonymous. Yes, they are connected, but they remain distinct. So if the Bible assumes that slavery is both a tolerable and inevitable institution, even explicitly saying that slaves are the property of slaveowners, that doesn't mean this is the Christian ethical position on slavery. Christianity is not a slave to the Bible—Christianity is a slave only to Christ! Out of the soil of Scripture grows a mature Christian faith that is not only able but required to oppose all forms of slavery in the name of Jesus.

Since the canon of Scripture is closed, the soil of the Christian faith is unchanging. But that doesn't prevent the living Christian faith itself from growing, changing, developing, and maturing over time. Of course, how it grows and changes will often be a matter of fervent debate within the church, but that's just the way it goes.

(And I understand that the deeply fractured nature of the church compounds the complexity of this problem.) The Bible may be stuck with the assumption that slavery is an inescapable institution, but the living faith of Christianity is capable of growth and can produce entire boughs of abolition.

To say that Christian faith is forever rooted in Scripture yet distinct from Scripture is both theologically conservative and theologically progressive: *conservative* in that it recognizes the inviolability of Scripture; *progressive* in that it makes a vital distinction between the living faith and the historic text. To say that the Christian faith is one and the same as the Bible is a fundamentalist mistake that is ultimately untenable. In the name of biblicism, you can wind up defending sin. I've encountered fundamentalists backed into a biblicist corner attempting to defend the Bible by saying, "Sometimes slavery is a good thing" and "There were good masters." And this was said in reference to American slavery! This is not defending the Bible; this is abusing the Bible! Regarding "good" slavery and "good" masters, James Cone writes,

> From the black perspective, the phrase "good" master is like speaking of "good" racists and "good" murderers. Who in their right minds could make such nonsensical distinctions, except those who deal in historical abstractions? Certainly not the victims! Indeed, it may be argued that the so-called good masters were in fact the worst, if we consider the dehumanizing effect of mental servitude. At least those who were blatant in their physical abuse did not camouflage their savagery with Christian doctrine, and it may have been easier for black slaves to make the necessary value-distinctions so that they could regulate their lives according to black definitions. But "good" Christian masters could cover up their brutality by rationalizing it with Christian theology, making it difficult for slaves to recognize the demonic. . . . The "good" master

convinced them that slavery was their lot ordained by God, and it was his will for blacks to be obedient to white people. After all, Ham was cursed, and St. Paul did admonish slaves to be obedient to their masters.[6]

When your biblical foundation requires you to defend the sin of slavery, it's time to get a new foundation!

THE ONLY PERFECT THEOLOGY

Let me be clear, I love the Bible. My theology is firmly rooted in the sacred soil of Scripture. I've read the Bible nearly every day for over four decades. The soil of Scripture is the primary source for the spiritual nutrients that permeate every area of my life. But my Christian faith is bigger than the Bible—and dare I say, better than the Bible. Jesus Christ is the only perfect theology and the only enduring foundation. In the end, I'm saying nothing more than what Jesus said when he spoke these words: "You search the Scriptures because you think that in them you have eternal life; and it is they that testify on my behalf. Yet you refuse to come to me to have life" (Jn 5:39-40). What the Bible does best, what the Bible does perfectly, what the Bible does infallibly is point us to Jesus as the Savior. Jesus saves the Bible from being an arcane religious text that can be misused to justify all manner of egregious evils, from slavery to crusades to colonialism. Ultimately it is Jesus—the only foundation!—who saves and sustains the Bible, the church, Christianity, and my faith.

My living faith began with a revelation of Jesus Christ when I was a teenager. Two years later, when I was a senior in high school, I wrote my senior paper on the resurrection of Jesus. I gave it the title "The Resurrection: Fact or Fiction?" I had become an eighteen-year-old Christian apologist. I worked very hard on that paper—an extremely rare occurrence for me in high school! My paper was informed by Josh McDowell's *Evidence That Demands a Verdict* and other similar books on Christian apologetics. If I remember correctly, I got an A—another rare occurrence. But I'm not proud of that paper. Why? Because it was disingenuous. My senior paper makes it sound like I believe in the resurrection of Jesus Christ because I had studied all the evidence and reached the only intelligent conclusion. But that's revisionist history.

I came to believe in the resurrection when Jesus was revealed to me on a Saturday night in 1974. And at that point, I didn't know a single apologetic argument for the historical resurrection—and I didn't need one! There may indeed be compelling reasons why the resurrection is the most feasible explanation for the empty tomb, *but that had nothing to do with my faith!* I believed in the resurrection before I ever heard of Josh McDowell. The foundation for my faith was not *Evidence That Demands a Verdict* but the evidence of my own experience. Yet as modern Christians, we are conditioned to be embarrassed by a claim to know something by a revelatory experience, so we are tempted to pretend that our faith is based on something everyone can agree on. But this is a departure from the apostolic understanding of how and why we believe in Jesus.

It's quite amazing to me that it took me decades to admit what I knew all along: I believe in Jesus because I *know* him. And today, I am not the least embarrassed to confess that the foundation for my faith is my own experience with the risen Christ. Amen.

I would like to bring this chapter to a close by sharing a letter I wrote to an atheist friend several years ago. He wanted to converse with a believer regarding faith, and I was happy to be his interlocutor. This is what I said.

LETTER TO AN ATHEIST

Dear Tim,

I agree with you about *The Case for Christ*. It's not a persuasive argument. Still, I would like to talk to you for a moment about

God. Not condescendingly, you deserve better than that, but from my heart. Please allow me to have my say.

Is there a God?

Yes and no.

"There" (the adverb denoting place and location) is no God. For God to be God, in the sense of an eternal, self-existent being responsible for all that we call existence, the one thing God cannot be is "there." God is of necessity invisible. There is a place called Timbuktu, there is a planet called Neptune, there is a cup of coffee sitting next to me, but in that sense, there is no God. That would be to place God within the universe as another object. That is what God cannot be. Unless God were to choose to in some way join creation. (This is what Christians believe concerning the incarnation of Christ, but that's another discussion.)

Can I prove that God exists? I don't think so, at least not in the way I might prove that I have three cats living at my house. I'm confident that God can prove his own existence, but he doesn't seem to be inclined to do so. At least not at the present moment. Though, without trying to persuade you to believe me, I do believe that God will, in his own time, erase all doubt of his reality from the mind of every intelligent being. But, as C. S. Lewis said, "When the author walks onto the stage, the play is over."

So "there" is no God.

But I believe God is.

Why?

Certainly not because I can make an ironclad argument for God's existence, but because I know that when I try my best to not believe in God, I know I am lying to myself.

Do I want there to be a God? Perhaps. But I can tell you what I want even more than the existence of God, and that is this: The Truth. And when I have experimented with thinking God out of existence, I know I have lied to myself. Is this a persuasive argument? Probably not for you. But it is for me. Perhaps the most persuasive. I know there is a God because I know there is a God. Circular? Yes. But I can't break out of the circle and remain true to myself. I can't unknow what I know and be true to myself. That's not much of an argument for believing in God, but I wanted to say it anyway. (Remember, I'm speaking from my heart.) On to other things.

An atheist doesn't believe in God. What doesn't an atheist believe in? God. Let us be absolutely clear on this point. What is it that an atheist is convinced doesn't exist? GOD. Hmm! Most atheists I have had conversations with seem to think about God nearly as much as I do. Most people don't believe in lots of things: Unicorns, Bigfoot, and the Loch Ness monster among them. But they don't bother to identify themselves as A-Bigfootists, etc. God is because God is. Even atheists know what God is. God is utterly unique. A class unto himself. This is the one thing God must be . . . or we wouldn't even have a word for it. Unicorns may be a fable, but there are horses and animals with horns. Bigfoot may not be in the woods, but there are large mammals in the woods. Nessie may not be in the loch, but there are strange creatures in the sea. But God is utterly unique—not a variation on a theme. To insist that one does not believe in God is an absurdity. (Strong words, but, yes, I believe that.) By the very use of the word you have acknowledged the reality of this utterly unique being. And so, as G. K. Chesterton quipped, "Without God there would be no atheists." I'm reminded of the recent debate at Oxford between Richard Dawkins and Alister McGrath and how Dawkins exclaimed during the debate, "My God!" Yes, the crowd laughed.

Here is a question. And, really, a serious one. Why is there something instead of nothing? We are here after all. Why? For a long time, the standard atheistic reply was something like, "Well, why not? That's just the way it is." In itself, that seems pretty weak, but then something happened that made that argument no longer tenable. The discovery of the Big Bang. We now know that 13.8 billion years ago, something happened that began time, space, and matter. Before that there was . . . well, nothing; nothing in the most literal sense of the word. There was not even a "before"—there was just nothing. And out of nothing—bang!—the beginning of time, space, and matter. Why?

Here is another question. What evidence would you accept as proof for the existence of God? What would you require of God to be persuaded of his existence? God would have to do what? Speak to you? (I'll get to that in a moment.) Appear to you? But then of course you could doubt the validity of this experience. Perhaps it's a hallucination. Or how would you know it's not an advanced alien with what appears, but only appears, to be divine attributes? How could God prove himself to you? Is there anything you cannot doubt? You know, it's possible to doubt even your own existence. So is one an atheist simply because it is impossible for one to believe that God is, no matter what evidence is presented? What if God did appear to you and you were convinced that God existed? How would you convince another human of God's reality? An interesting question to ponder.

Alright, back to Bigfoot. Suppose you knew me to be a generally truthful person. And suppose I told you that there was a Bigfoot living in the woods behind my house. And suppose that several other generally reliable people told you the same thing. And suppose they said that if you were to go investigate the woods yourself, that although they could not guarantee that you would see Bigfoot, they nevertheless stated there was a high probability that you would see Bigfoot for yourself . . . wouldn't you at least bother to go have a look? In other words, these generally truthful people were not merely asking you to take their word for it but were asking you to investigate the situation yourself. Wouldn't you do it?

I would like to tell you about the woods where I think you might possibly find God.

Prayer.

Pray to God and see if anything happens. Ask God if he is real, and if so, to, in some fashion, let you know. Ask sincerely, even though you will of course ask skeptically. What have you to lose?

You at least know that there are intelligent, sincere people who claim to have met God in the woods of prayer. Perhaps they are mistaken, but why not examine the experience yourself?

Is it scary to meet Bigfoot in the woods? I can only imagine. Is it scary to encounter God in reality? I have found it (and many other things) so. The implications are enormous. But when I told you that what I want more than anything is the Truth, I told the truth. Of course, I may be an evil alien out to deceive you, who knows? For everything can be doubted. We all make decisions based on faith all day long.

I will not directly try to convince you that God is. Even though I have raised these questions, I think it is beyond my ability to convince anyone of God's existence. And neither do I really feel it is my job to do so. But I will point out the woods where many people claim to have met God. And some of them were what you would call very reliable people.

Prayer.

I think it's worth a look.

Tim, these are not patronizing words. I respect you. I respect you as a fellow human being, a genuine seeker, and as a remarkably intelligent man. I am simply sharing with you my experience with God. And I do so in the hope that you might have a similar experience. It's not really an argument I am offering (though I have made some weak points and raised a few questions). What I am offering is the possibility of an experience. No guarantees, but the possibility of (as unlikely as it may seem!) experiencing God.

I wish you all the best.

Your friend,

Brian Zahnd

8

ALL ALONE
UPSTAIRS

T he modern technological age we have inherited had its
  beginning with a seventeenth-century European intellectual
movement emphasizing reason and individualism over faith and
tradition, and René Descartes (1596–1650), as much as any other
figure, can be considered the father of this movement we call the
Enlightenment. His philosophical proposition *Cogito, ergo sum* (I
think, therefore I am) remains one of the most famous axioms in
the history of Western thought. If we had to give a symbolic date
for the beginning of the Enlightenment, we could probably
connect it with the publication of Descartes's *Discourse on Method*
in 1637. Few books have altered the course of history more decisively than this seminal work.

   But the Enlightenment's emphasis on reason and individualism over and against faith and tradition placed enormous
pressure on the church and especially the medieval Scholas-
ticism that had dominated universities since Thomas Aquinas.
Many people, then and now, see the Enlightenment as an attack

on the Christian faith. Paradoxically, this was something that Descartes, a lifelong devout Catholic, did *not* intend. In fact, in a letter to his publisher Descartes explained that one of the primary purposes of *Discourse on Method* was to logically prove the existence of God.

But as we have already seen, once we accept the challenge to prove the existence of God according to the terms that we would prove the existence of any other contingent object or phenomenon in the universe, we have stepped into an arena where atheism is bound to prevail. The very rules of the game make this a foregone conclusion. If God is the ground of being ("For in him we live and move and have our being" [Acts 17:28 KJV]), then we should not think of God as a *thing* in the universe whose existence is to be proved in the same way that we would prove the existence of, say, a giant squid.

Descartes was attempting to find a philosophical foundation on which he could build everything (including logical proof of the existence of God). He went about this project by attempting to dig deeper and deeper until he found philosophical bedrock in the form of that which cannot be doubted. In *Discourse on Method*, Descartes explains it like this:

> For a long time I had observed that in practical life it is sometimes necessary to act upon opinions which one knows to be quite uncertain just as if they were indubitable. But since I now wished to devote myself to the search for truth, I thought it necessary to do the very opposite and reject as if absolutely false everything in which I could imagine the least doubt, in order to see if I was left believing anything that was entirely indubitable. . . . I resolved to pretend that all the things that had ever entered my mind were no more true than the illusions of my dreams. But immediately I noticed that while I was trying thus to think everything false, it was necessary that

I, who was thinking this, was something. And observing that
this truth *I am thinking, therefore I exist* was so firm and sure
that all the most extravagant suppositions of the sceptics
were incapable of shaking it, I decided that I could accept it
without scruple as the first principle of the philosophy I
was seeking.[1]

Descartes had found what he regarded as philosophical bedrock,
and he had also effectively established the autonomous thinking
individual (as opposed to faith and tradition) as the ultimate arbiter of truth. A rigid dualism was established between superior
rational thought and all lesser means of knowing. Theologian
Elizabeth Johnson says,

> At the dawn of the modern era the ancient tree of hierarchical
> dualism received a new layer of foliage in the philosophy of
> René Descartes. As he saw it, the world is divided into human
> rational mind which knows (*res cogitans*) and all other things
> which are objects of knowledge (*res extensa*).[2]

Cogito, ergo sum may be an adequate foundation for a scientific
method sufficient for understanding the natural world and capable of creating the technology to put a man on the moon and
invent the internet. But is all of reality limited to what can be inves-
tigated in the scientific method? Is the whole of reality contained
in what can be experienced through the five physical sense organs?
Can being itself be accounted for in the syllogisms of the logician?
One thinks here of the humble caution of Ludwig Wittgenstein as
he concludes his famous *Tractatus*—"What we cannot speak about
we must pass over in silence."[3]

I'm not a philosopher, so I'll leave the critique of the limita-
tions of "I think, therefore I am" to Søren Kierkegaard, Martin
Heidegger, John MacMurray, and others, but I will point out that
if one of Descartes's aims was to prove the existence of God, he

had, in fact, taken a course that makes God unknowable. "I think, therefore I am" *may* be an adequate epistemological foundation for scientific inquiry, but theologically, it's a move that leaves us all alone upstairs inside our head. If we intend to purely *think* our way to God, the more likely result is crippling skepticism. As Kierkegaard points out, "When thinking turns toward itself in order to think about itself, there emerges, as we know, a skepticism."[4] If we privilege the head over the heart in *all* matters of inquiry, we may very well cut ourselves off from that which is intellectually unknowable. The rational mind is capable of amazing accomplishments, but it is not an organ suitable for experiencing God. Attempting to use the rational mind as the organ for experiencing God is rather like trying to smell a rose with your ear. The ear is a remarkable sense organ, but it's not the organ for experiencing aroma. We cannot perceive with the mind those things that the heart alone is capable of perceiving. And that leads us to Descartes's contemporary and intellectual equal Blaise Pascal.

The label *genius* may be thrown around too freely, but it certainly applies to Blaise Pascal (1623–1662). He was a mathematical savant who reportedly as a twelve-year-old boy discovered for himself the first thirty-two propositions of Euclid's *Elements* and went on to become one of the most celebrated mathematicians and physicists in history. But Pascal's interests and experiences were not confined to the mathematical and scientific. Following a dramatic conversion at age thirty-one, what he referred to as his "night of fire," Pascal also become one of the most celebrated religious thinkers of his era. He wrote the account of his night of fire on a piece of parchment that he carried with him for the rest of his life. In part, the parchment reads,

THE MEMORIAL

The year of grace 1654

Monday, 23 November

*From about half past ten in the evening until half
      past midnight.*

Fire!

*God of Abraham, God of Isaac, God of Jacob, not of
      philosophers and scholars.*

Certainty, certainty, heartfelt, joy, peace.

God of Jesus Christ.

God of Jesus Christ.

My God and your God.

Thy God shall be my God.

The world forgotten, and everything except God.

He can only be found by the ways taught in the Gospels.

Greatness of the human soul.

*O righteous Father, the world had not known thee,
      but I have known thee.*

Joy, joy, joy, tears of joy.

Everlasting joy in return for one day's effort on earth.

I will not forget thy word. Amen.[5]

As a preeminent mathematician and inventor of the precursor to the modern computer, Pascal understood the potential and value of the rational mind. One cannot accuse Pascal of dismissing reason. But after his mystical night of fire, Pascal understood the limits of reason. By employing the rational mind, someone might invent a calculating machine (as Pascal did), but the rational mind is not the means by which we encounter God. Pascal could not mathematically prove his mystical experience with God, but he knew it was true and had his "Memorial" sewn into his clothing. In *Pensées*, a collection of spiritual reflections published after his death, Pascal wrote, "The heart has its reasons of which reason knows nothing: we know this in countless ways. . . . It is the heart which perceives God and not the reason. That is what faith is: God perceived by the heart, not by reason."[6]

THE LEAP TO FAITH

The heart has its reasons that though incomprehensible to the rational mind are entirely legitimate. Empiricism is fine until it becomes haughty and claims it can know everything that can be known. As an organ for experiencing and interpreting reality, the heart is not inferior to reason. Just as you cannot hear with your tongue or smell with your ear, so the experience of God is not a phenomenon of the mind but of the heart. Theology is an activity of the mind, but the *experience* of God belongs to the heart. The less intelligent and less educated are at no disadvantage in experiencing God. The potential to know and experience God is truly egalitarian. Like Pascal, I'm not at all against reason. I just know that it has its limits and cannot accomplish what it is ontologically incapable of doing.

It's proper and legitimate to be upstairs inside your head when you're doing geometry, attempting to calculate the circumference of the earth, designing microprocessors, or trying to understand the nature of dark matter, but it's not where you will meet God. God will not be encountered all alone upstairs in our head; we meet God downstairs in the living room—in our heart. And by *heart*, I don't mean the realm of sentiment but that part of our being where we experience such phenomenon as love. The pure empiricist will tell us that what we experience as love is nothing more than a chemical response advantageous to our evolutionary development. But though we may readily acknowledge that chemical responses are present in the experience of certain kinds of love, very few of us are willing to say that love is nothing but hormones and neurons. We simply know better. To live in a world where love does not exist would be to live in hell—and that may be very close to what hell is: a world where love is not real.

Modernity insists that we live alone upstairs inside our head. Modernity rejects faith and claims that the heart is inferior to the mind in evaluating experience. Modernity scoffs at tradition as a superstitious relic to be discarded in an age of reason. Well, allow me to tell you that you have postmodern permission to tell modernity to get off its high horse and shut up.

Modernity may want to pretend that it stands above tradition as "pure reason," but in fact it's just a tradition of critiquing and ultimately rejecting all other traditions. And as such, it's a rather impoverished tradition. Contrary to the propaganda of modernity, not all tradition is founded on superstition and motivated by a desire to control people. Unhealthy tradition may have those characteristics, and this is the kind of tradition that Jesus critiqued, but tradition is also how wisdom (especially moral and spiritual wisdom) is passed on from generation to generation. To reject all tradition *simply because it is tradition* is juvenile folly.

As for modernity's claim that the heart is an illegitimate means of evaluating reality, you already know this claim is bogus; you may have just been afraid to say so. The heart knows what it knows. Allow me or any number of reliable witnesses to permit you to affirm the truth in Pascal's wise aphorism: "The heart indeed has its reasons of which reason knows nothing." You don't have to stay upstairs inside your head. Come downstairs, into your heart, into the living room, and experience the love of God. As the apostle Paul says, let Christ dwell in your heart by faith (Eph 3:17). Faith is not a feeling; faith is not empirical proof. Faith is *action* based on that which is revealed to the heart. Make a decision and take what Kierkegaard calls the leap into faith. (The correct phrase is not a leap *of* faith but a leap *to* faith.) By this, Kierkegaard means that

Christian faith is the *decision* to *act* in imitation of Jesus Christ because in your heart you know this is right. Here's how Kierkegaard explains it:

> Without a life of imitation, of following Christ, it is impossible to gain mastery over doubts. We cannot stop doubt with reasons. Those who try have not learned that it is wasted effort. . . . The Savior of the world did not come to bring a doctrine; he never lectured. He did not try by way of reasons to prevail upon anyone to accept his teaching. . . . If someone wanted to be his follower, he said to that person something like this, "Venture a decisive act; then you can begin, then you will know." . . . This is the only proof possible for the truth of what he represents: "If anyone will act according to what I say, he will experience whether I am speaking on my own." . . . Yes, doubt will come, even to the one who follows Christ. But the only person who has a right to leap forward even with a doubt is someone whose life bears the marks of imitation, someone who by a decisive action at least tries to go so far out that becoming a Christian can still be a possibility. Everyone else must hold his tongue; he has no right to put in a word about Christianity; least of all *contra*.[7]

To live a Christian life is an inherently risky venture. To base the course of your life on attempting to follow Jesus entails the gamble that either Jesus is Lord or you are wasting your life. Paul said it this way: "If Christ has not been raised, your faith is futile. . . . If for this life only we have hoped in Christ, we are of all people most to be pitied" (1 Cor 15:17, 19). Because true Christian faith is not merely holding a particular theological opinion but a life you actually live, the stakes are high. But this is a risk that Christianity requires. Commenting on Kierkegaard's leap to faith, Kierkegaard scholar Charles E. Moore writes:

Faith, therefore, requires a leap. It is not a matter of galvanizing the will to believe something there is no evidence for, but a leap of commitment. "The leap is a category of decision"—the decision to commit one's being totally to a God whose existence is rationally uncertain and whose redemption is utterly an offense. This is why, according to Kierkegaard, all proofs for the existence of God and the deity of Christ fail. To try and prove God's existence by means of a purely neutral, objective standpoint is completely backwards. . . . To the contrary, God is known by way of a passionate, undivided commitment.[8]

PEACHES AND LIONS

We have bought the lie that the way to encounter truth is to remain objective (as if such objectivity is even possible). No! All truth inheres or exists in subjectivity. The only truth that matters is the truth you live.[9] Jesus is the Truth, not because of the opinions he objectively held in his head but because of the life he lived. Faith is the decision to act on the truth apprehended in your heart. When Jesus first revealed himself to me when I was fifteen, I began to live a different life—this alone can be called faith. Faith is not producing a sense of certainty about God in our thinking. If all we ever do is *think* about God, we will end up overridden with doubt. The practice of *only* thinking about God is an incubator of atheism. We first encounter Christ in revelation, and then in response to this revelation, we *worship* Christ, we *obey* Christ, we *follow* Christ—this alone is faith. When we seek to understand and explain what we have encountered, this is theology—faith seeking understanding. But theology must be rooted in the faith action of actually seeking to worship and obey God. If we only approach God objectively or academically, we will never really know God and our theology will be mistaken and misleading. Perhaps an illustration will help.

Imagine a person who is the world's foremost expert on peaches. He has learned all that can be objectively learned about peaches— their genus, subgenus, species, the trees that produce them, their history, cultivation, and varieties, even the sequence of their DNA. Imagine that this man, we'll call him Dr. Prunus Persica, has written dozens of scholarly works on peaches, given countless university lectures on peaches, and has received numerous academic awards for his work in the scientific understanding of peaches. No one knows more about peaches than Dr. Persica. But now imagine that for some bizarre, inexplicable reason Dr. Persica has never actually *eaten* a peach.

Does Dr. Persica *really* know more about peaches than a child who has eaten a peach? The real truth—the truth that matters—about peaches is known by subjective experience. It is fine and even commendable to have objective academic knowledge about peaches, but this is not what peaches are *for*. The purpose of peaches is not to be studied but to be eaten and enjoyed. Dr. Persica can speak far more learnedly about peaches, but it is the three-year-old girl who eats a perfect Georgia peach in July who actually *knows* peaches! Trying to know God *objectively*—all alone inside your heard—is like trying to know peaches without eating them.

The psalmist writes, "Oh, taste and see that the LORD is good!" (Ps 34:8 ESV). *Oh* is the word of subjectivity—it indicates that we *feel* something, that we *experience* something. The theologian who writes about God but never utters *Oh, God* in prayer is not a theologian I'm interested in. The apostle Paul is never more the theologian than in his three chapter discourse on election in Romans 9–11. Paul sums up his dense theological argument by saying, "God has imprisoned all in disobedience so that he may be merciful to all" (Rom 11:32). But then Paul breaks into an ecstatic doxology: "Oh, the depth of the riches and wisdom and knowledge of God!" (Rom 11:33). Paul has the objective rigorous intellect of a great theologian, but he also has the subjective *Oh* of someone who truly experiences God. Paul's objective theology that he places on parchment ultimately lives and moves and has its being in subjective experience.

We've spoken of peaches, now let's move on to lions. When the subject is God (and God is the eternal Subject!), trying to know God objectively is how we play it safe. It's like the steel bars on the lion cage in the zoo. We go to the zoo, we see the lions, we may be impressed, but there is little genuine passion because we know we are perfectly safe—we will never actually encounter the lions. But petting a lion is an entirely different experience! You cannot pet a lion and be objective about it. And I *have* petted a full-grown male lion—it's an experience I won't forget!

Here's my point: academic theology *can* be like the bars of the lion's cage—it keeps our experience of God objective, prosaic, safe, undemanding. I say this as a person who deeply appreciates academic theology. I've read hundreds of academic theological works, and, occasionally, I give theological lectures in academic settings. I view these as valuable endeavors. But none of it is to be confused with the experience of encountering God subjectively. Subjective experience with the divine is a phenomenon that occurs within a heart that is open to God: "Blessed are the pure in heart, for they will see God" (Mt 5:8). But the intellect *can* be employed as the steel bars that keep us a safe distance from the lion.

The famous Jesus Seminar is an academic group composed of biblical scholars who get together to vote on which of the verses in the Gospels reflect the historic words and deeds of the historic Jesus. They do this with the use of colored beads—red, pink, gray, black. Red means "for sure," and black means "no way." Pink and gray are somewhere in between. Well, the Jesus Seminar can vote with their beads on whether or not Jesus preached the Sermon on the Mount or rose from the dead, but that's mostly just trying to cage the lion. The steel bars (or colored beads) of alleged objectivity keep us at a safe distance from what the words and deeds of Jesus demand of us.

The Jesus Seminar is following the lead of German philosopher Gotthold Lessing, who thought that historical distance prevents us from encountering Jesus Christ. Lessing called this historical distance "the ugly broad ditch." But steel bars, colored beads, and ugly broad ditches are just ways of keeping Jesus at a safe "objective" distance. If you honestly want to encounter Jesus, here's what I recommend: read the Gospels on your knees for six months, asking Jesus before each chapter to reveal himself to you. Seriously, try it. Don't be surprised if you eventually find yourself inside the cage face-to-face with the Lion of Judah. Then you'll have to decide what to do with your life now that you've gone through the wardrobe, entered Narnia, and encountered the real Aslan.

Jesus is clear that the only way to know if his teaching is from God is a resolve to act. "Anyone who resolves to do the will of God will know whether the teaching is from God or whether I am speaking on my own" (Jn 7:17). You'll never know if Jesus is the way, the truth, and the life by sitting all alone upstairs in your head thinking about it. You have to act on it. This is how you jump Lessing's ditch. This is precisely what the leap to faith is all about. Kierkegaard knew about Lessing's ditch, and he also knew how to get across it. Leap!

In *Unfading Light*, the highly creative and influential Orthodox theologian Sergius Bulgakov, after a prolonged period as a Marxist atheist, beautifully describes his return to Christian faith as a leap to faith:

> In my theoretical strivings and doubts a single motif, one secret hope, now sounded in me all the clearer—the question *What if?* And what began burning in my soul for the first time since the days in the Caucasus became all the more

imperious and bright; but the main thing was all the more definite: I did not need a "philosophical" idea of Divinity but a living faith in God, in Christ and the Church. *If* it is true that there is a God, this *means* that everything that was given to me in childhood but which I had abandoned is true. Such was the semi-conscious religious syllogism that my soul made: nothing . . . or everything, everything down to the last little candle, the last little icon. And the work of my soul went on nonstop, invisible to the world and unclear even to me. What happened on a wintery Moscow street, in a crowded square, is memorable—suddenly a miraculous flame of faith began burning in my soul, my heart beat, tears of joy dimmed my eyes. In my soul "the will to believe" ripened, the resolution finally to carry through with the leap to the other shore, so senseless for the wisdom of the world, from Marxism and every *ism* resulting from it to . . . Orthodoxy. Oh, yes, of course it is a leap, towards happiness and joy; an abyss lies between both shores. *I had to* jump.[10]

Thirteen years before I read Sergius Bulgakov's account of his leap to faith, I had a similar experience. I had reached a point in midlife where I was either going to yield to spiritual complacency or I had to make some decisive and risky moves to live a life of passionate commitment to Christ. During that time, I wrote a poem I titled "LEAP!" When trying to communicate the nature of a spiritual experience, poetry is sometimes a more reliable vehicle than prose.

LEAP!

And shall I go on being casual and numb?
Pretending
Pretending that I know something about this being I so
*   glibly call God*
Or shall I dare to encounter Him?

Him

The One with whom I have to do

The One who can never be an object

Forever and always the eternal subject

Is it grammar or a much deeper truth?

The object is acted upon but the subject acts

God is not in my story—I am in His

How is it I can be unaware of this?

Did I think I invented this story called being?

Surely I'm not that crazy

I belong to His story

History

But there is my story

Mystery

God is no object—only and ever a subject

The Subject

You cannot trivialize The Subject to ology or ism

You can only be aware or oblivious

Of the One who alone possesses innate beingness

The most obvious of all truth

But all truth inheres in subjectivity

Oh!

Subjectivity

Where passion is permitted

Where we are in the story

Where we care

Instead of aloof and comfortably numb

Subjectivity is passion

Faith is passion

Life is passion

Sanity is passion

Objectivity is numb

Empiricism is numb
Death is numb
Madness is numb
Passion saves
My soul
From numbness
Prose
Prozac
Prosaic
Ordinary
Medicated
Unimaginative
Passionless being
Passion saves
Poetic prophetic extraordinary imaginative
Passionate being
Passion saves
To believe is to be passionate
Passion is found in the instant of the leap
When you leap beyond the fence
(Objectivity)
Into the Lion's presence
(Subjectivity)
Will He kill you or let you live?
Either way you are alive at that moment
You are not cool or "cool"
One is dispassionate the other is self-conscious
At that moment you are neither
You are passionate and engaged
LEAP!
The security barrier of objectivity
Into the presence of the Being Himself

It's the only hope you have of saving your life
Leprosy is not what you think it is
It doesn't eat you
It's only numbness
But numbness will destroy you
LEAP!
Before it's too late
Before the leprosy takes your legs away
Before the creeping numbness takes your soul away
LEAP!
The Leap to faith
That jumps the objective
To encounter the Subject
Where passion lives
Because now there is nothing between you and the Lion
And you know you live because you feel your heartbeat
And you know you live because He lets you live
No more numbness
Passion saves
LEAP!

PART 2

FAITH FORGED FROM THE ASHES

A MYSTIC OR NOTHING AT ALL

The devout Christian of the future will
either be a "mystic," one who has "experienced"
something, or he will cease to be anything at all.

KARL RAHNER, "CHRISTIAN LIVING FORMERLY AND TODAY"

In 1971, three centuries after Blaise Pascal observed that the heart has its reasons of which reason knows nothing, Karl Rahner, a German Catholic priest and theologian, predicted that the Christian of the future will be a mystic or nothing at all. By "mystic," we simply mean a person who seeks and at some level attains *a direct experience within the mystery of God.* And Karl Rahner was correct about the future of Christianity lying with the mystics. Half a century later, Rahner's prophecy feels more prescient than ever.

Religion that resides solely in the intellect is incapable of sustaining faith in our disenchanted age. In a secular epoch, the Christian will either be a mystic or nothing at all. The tsunami of secularism scouring Western Europe and North America will not abate anytime soon. This spiritual crisis will not be survived by clever apologetics or by waging misguided culture wars or by pining away for an irretrievable past. If the Christian faith is to survive the tsunami of secularism, it will be because Christians have their own *experience* with God. The faith of the future will be sustained by an experience, not an argument. As the old saying goes, a person with an experience is not at the mercy of a person with an argument.

Because we are all children of God created in the image of God, we are all capable of experiencing God. The experience of God is a possibility inherent to our nature. Birds can fly, fish can swim, and humans can experience God. It *is* possible to encounter, experience, and enjoy the God who created and loves us. We can all be mystics—we were made for it. Famous mystics like Francis of Assisi, Hildegard von Bingen, Julian of Norwich, Teresa of Ávila, John of the Cross, and Thomas Merton were spiritual savants. But they are also reliable witnesses and trusted guides for what to some extent is accessible to all of us. In 1970, the Roman Catholic Church declared Teresa of Ávila a Doctor of the Church—one who has made a significant contribution to theology and is regarded as especially reliable. Declaring this sixteenth-century Carmelite nun and Spanish mystic a Doctor of the Church was an important affirmation of the theology of Christian mysticism. At the time, Karl Rahner said, "Teresa is proclaimed as a teacher of mysticism. This means first of all that a person who teaches something about mysticism is doing theology, is speaking in the light of revelation, saying something to the Church as such for the edification of the faithful."[1]

It is no accident that Teresa was declared a Doctor of the Church at the same time that the charismatic movement was sweeping through Catholic and Protestant churches around the world. Karl Rahner affirmingly described the charismatic movement as "mysticism for the masses."[2] Charismatic Christianity was a movement in which tongues, prophecy, visions, healing, and energetic worship were normative spiritual experiences. The charismatic movement was a fresh wind blowing away the dust and cobwebs within a moribund church.

One of the most remarkable aspects of the charismatic movement was how it was experienced throughout the entire ecumenical spectrum. My spiritual roots are in the Jesus movement and charismatic renewal of the 1970s. I remember well the thrill of discovering this "mysticism for the masses." I remember well Catholics and Baptists joyfully attending the same charismatic meetings. In July 1977, fifty thousand people from every facet of the body of Christ attended the Charismatic Renewal Conference held at Arrowhead Stadium in Kansas City, Missouri. Around the world, millions of people for whom Christianity was little more than a nominal identity or a tedious duty were suddenly filled with the Holy Spirit, discovering a Christianity characterized by the joy and excitement of actually experiencing God. Yes, the movement was rambunctious and unwieldy, and, as is always the case in such movements, there were excesses. But on the whole, the charismatic movement rescued Christianity for millions of people who were on the verge of accepting modernity's indictment that Christianity was nothing more than an arcane relic of the past.

The eventual decline and demise of the charismatic movement—at least within the Protestant world—was not due to its sometimes silly excesses but to its capitulation to American consumerism in the form of the prosperity gospel propagated by celebrity televangelists. When the charismatic movement became more about

money than miracles, the Holy Spirit left and the movement de-
cayed. But for a time, it was the wonderful and healthy experience
of coming to see the mystical as attainable and normative. It's this
kind of mysticism that we should pursue.

Mysticism is not a freakish outlier on the far edge of Christianity
or the exclusive domain for a rare elite. The mystical life is the
normal Christian life. At the birth of the church on the day of Pentecost, "All of them were filled with the Holy Spirit and began to
speak in other languages, as the Spirit gave them ability" (Acts 2:4).
At the conclusion of his Pentecost sermon, the apostle Peter told
the assembled crowd that the experience of the Holy Spirit was for
everyone: "The promise is for you, for your children, and for all
who are far away, everyone whom the Lord our God calls to him"
(Acts 2:39). For you, for all, for everyone. From the very outset,
Christianity has viewed the mystical experience of the Spirit as uni-
versally available. No one who has studied the rise of early Christianity can deny that charismatic experience among common
people was a key component to its improbable success. And it
should be pointed out that today Pentecostal Christianity is easily
the fastest growing expression of global Christianity.

As Western culture races away from the sacred and sacramental
into the secular and technological, it leaves masses of humanity
yearning for the possibility of some kind of transcendent experience that can alert us to the truth that life has meaning and
purpose. Commenting on Karl Rahner's view of mysticism, Rahner
translator Annemarie Kidder writes, "Mysticism helps recover the
presence of God in the world and in everyday life; it makes intel-
ligible the personal experience with God, unmasks false God experiences, and allows God's presence to emerge where one might
have overlooked or ignored it."[3]

We might be tempted to paraphrase Rahner's remark and say
that the Christian of the future will be at least somewhat

Pentecostal. Christian mysticism isn't rooted in new age spirituality but in the Pentecostal experience found in the second chapter of Acts.

MYSTICS IN THE BIBLE

The Bible itself is a mystical book—it was produced by Jewish and Christian mystics filled with the Holy Spirit. The texts that became sacred Scripture did not come from people who were merely *thinking* about God but from people who had a direct *experience* with God. Those who wrote the Bible were not scholars but mystics. It's significant to note that *all* of the most important figures in the Bible are men and women with stories of mystical experience.

Abraham was a mystic who discerned the voice of God and followed that voice away from the dumb idols of Chaldea and into a relationship with the living God. This mystic became the father of faith.

Jacob was a mystic who wrestled with God and gained a new identity. This mystic was given the mystical name Israel—one who strives with God and prevails.

Moses was a mystic whose life was changed when he perceived God in a bush on fire with the divine presence and climbed Mount Sinai to talk with God face-to-face. This mystic liberated the people of Israel.

David was a mystic. The one who was called "the man after God's own heart" (1 Sam 13:14) was not the bloody warrior but the mystical psalmist. This mystic was the righteous king who wrote psalms beside moonlit streams.

Elijah was a mystic—the archetypal prophet who hears from God and speaks for God. This mystic who challenged the prophets of Baal is the pinnacle of the Hebrew prophetic tradition.

Mary the mother of Jesus was a mystic who had the ultimate direct encounter with God. This mystic gave flesh to the Logos and became the *Theotokos*—"the God-bearer."

Peter was a mystic who was the first disciple to receive the revelation that Jesus is the Christ, the Son of the living God. This mystic with the keys of the kingdom opened the door of salvation for both the Jewish and Gentile worlds.

John was a mystic who laid his head on the breast of Jesus at the Last Supper and heard the divine heartbeat. This mystic gave us the zenith of theological mysticism in his Gospel.

Mary Magdalene was a mystic delivered from seven demons who followed Jesus more faithfully than any other disciple. This mystic was the first to encounter the risen Christ and became the apostle to the apostles.

Paul was a mystic who received his gospel through a direct encounter with the risen Christ. This mystic became the most successful apostle and most important theologian in the history of Christianity.

These biblical mystics may be exceptional in their unique contributions, but they are also patterns for all of us. We too can be mystics who encounter God, follow God, wrestle with God, speak to and for God, compose prayers, open new doors, hear the divine heartbeat, proclaim the gospel, and, most importantly, give flesh to the Word of God in our own lives. Mystical experiences are not foreign to scriptural tradition but are the norm within scriptural tradition. These mystics found in Scripture—and I only mentioned ten, there are many more—are witnesses to the possibility of mystical experiences in our own lives. If all we do is read about father Abraham and King David, the Virgin Mary and Mary Magdalene and never open our hearts to our own experiences, we have become history readers instead of God-seekers. The Bible is not just giving us mere information; it is hinting at portals that can lead to our own spiritual experiences. The Christian mystics of the future will relate to the biblical patriarchs and matriarchs, apostles and prophets because in their own way they have had similar experiences.

PERSONAL EXPERIENCES WITH THE MYSTICAL

The goal of spiritual practices like prayer, worship, scripture reading, and the like is to become properly formed as a being who bears the *imago Dei*—the image of God. Thus, the primary purpose of prayer is not to get God to do what we want God to do but to be properly formed—to become the person God created us to be. In my own life, I've been formed spiritually and theologically to a surprising degree by mystical experiences.

Academic theology and spiritual mysticism do not need to be pitted against one another; they are, in fact, entirely compatible. Over the years, I've been diligent to become thoroughly acquainted with the long history of Christian theology, and I'm convinced my theology has developed within the confines of historic orthodoxy, but I also testify that my spiritual formation is shaped as much by mystical experiences as by theological studies. When I speak of mystical experiences, I'm referring to approximately two dozen experiences scattered over more than forty-five years. These are not common occurrences, but they have had an outsized influence on the trajectory of my life.

The first experience was encountering the presence of Jesus in my bedroom in the form of pure light on the night of November 9, 1974. Another experience was waking up speaking in tongues—when I didn't believe in speaking in tongues! One was a word of faith after receiving a grim medical diagnosis when I was eighteen. Another experience is what I would call an angelic presence when I was in a car accident. Six of these experiences were dreams—one of them a recurring dream.

Of course, I've had countless dreams that may have had some spiritual significance at the time, but six of them, I have never forgotten. All six dreams either helped clarify a theological problem I was wrestling with or encouraged me during a difficult time. In one dream, I experienced my death and a glimpse of the world beyond death. It was peaceful and comforting. In another dream, Jesus appeared to me. It was so powerful, so real, and so significant that I can't describe it as a dream *about* Jesus but as Jesus *appearing* to me in a dream. One was a vision of a sin I had committed years previously—a sin that I didn't even know was a sin. This led to deep repentance and pivotal change in my theology regarding Christian participation in war.[4] A couple of experiences occurred while sitting with Jesus in contemplative prayer. They helped me to look at difficult situations and adversaries in the transforming light of love.

I don't think my experiences with the mystical are rare or exceptional; I think *most* people have similar experiences. But we may have been conditioned through secular or religious empiricism to ignore or deny these experiences. We may simply need to be more open to spiritual experiences and pay more attention to how God is present in our lives. Contemplative prayer is largely the practice of paying attention to God deeply and deliberately. This is necessary because we live in such a spiritually distracted age.

The largest category of my mystical experiences are words from the Lord—some of them found in Scripture, some of them not. Words such as:

- ◆ I shall not die but live and declare the works of the Lord.

- ◆ I believe I will see the goodness of God in the land of the living.

- ◆ Preach faith and your church will grow.

- ◆ I will help you.

- ◆ Come with me.

- ◆ This is the greatest wonder of all: the Word became flesh.

- ◆ Read this book.

- ◆ Cross, Mystery, Eclectic, Community, Revolution.

- ♦ Pay attention to every crucifix and ask this question: What does this mean?

- ♦ In one experience when there were no words, but I heard the Lord laugh.

These ten oracles only amount to about seventy words in all—they are words, phrases, short sentences at most. Some of them came as thunder in my soul, and some came as gentle whispers. They are not lengthy; they are not prophecies or Epistles. But these words have had an almost incalculable influence on the course of my life, my ministry, and my theology. I realize the dubious will be unimpressed, dismissing my mystical experiences as nothing more than having a few thoughts in my head. But these experiences were not mere thoughts or ideas. I have thoughts and ideas all the time; I know what that common everyday experience is like. These experiences were not that. These words did not originate in my thinking but came to me from elsewhere. These were not fleeting thoughts that came and went but words I have never forgotten. These oracles were not the transient flowers of my imagination. These were inspired words that came from without, entered within, and are now a permanent part of who I am. These words have never faded away. "The grass withers, the flower fades, But the word of our God stands forever" (Is 40:8 NASB).

In some of these cases, perhaps most, I didn't fully realize at the time how important these words were. It was only as time went by and these words settled deep into my soul, began to take root, and eventually produced fruit that I realized how special they were. A humanly generated thought and a divinely inspired word are simply not the same thing. "The words of the LORD are pure words, like silver refined from ore and purified seven times in the fire" (Ps 12:6 BCP). One word from God can change your life forever. Over time you can learn the difference between a word that originates in your head and a word that truly comes from the Lord. The prophet Isaiah, speaking on behalf of Yahweh, says:

> For my thoughts are not your thoughts,
>> Nor are your ways my ways, says the LORD.
> For as the heavens are higher than the earth,
>> so are my ways higher than your ways
>> and my thoughts than your thoughts.
> For as the rain and the snow come down from heaven,
>> and do not return there until they have watered the earth,
> making it bring forth and sprout,
>> giving seed to the sower and bread to the eater,
> so shall my word be that goes out of my mouth;
>> it shall not return to me empty,
> but it shall accomplish that which I purpose,
>> and succeed in the thing for which I sent it. (Is 55:8-11)

Sometimes the word of the Lord comes to us like rain, and it immediately brings refreshing. Other times, the word of the Lord comes like snow, and it is only later, as time goes by and the snow begins to melt, that we experience the influence of the word sent from heaven. Whether as rain or snow, how I thank God for these words more precious than gold that have been granted to me throughout my life. They've healed me, helped me, encouraged me, kept me in my vocation, led me into new paths, and given me new and better ways of thinking about God. Where I am today—spiritually and theologically—is not just the result of reading good theological works (though that is important) but also the result of timely words from heaven received in a mystical moment that put me on the right path. "Your ears shall hear a word behind you, saying, 'This is the way; walk in it'" (Is 30:21).

I allude to some of my own experiences with the mystical not to lay claim to spiritual elitism but to bear witness to the normality of such experiences. I think most Christians have had similar experiences, but in modernity, we have been conditioned to be hesitant to talk about them lest we be embarrassed before our secular and skeptical friends. We should let go of that embarrassment.

I'm not advocating religious fanaticism (which is a real malady) or encouraging spiritual boasting (which *should* embarrass us) but simply stating that a personal witness to a direct experience with God is nothing to be embarrassed about. I've found that most people are interested in the stories of our personal experience with the divine. Most people hope that God can be experienced, and our testimonies of mystical experience enliven that hope.

For those who hope for mystical experiences, I have some advice. First, don't seek a mystical experience; seek God. I've never had a mystical experience by seeking a mystical experience. Let God be God, and don't make an idol out of mystical experiences. Seeking mystical experiences is to flirt with idolatry that often leads to the destructive phenomena of spiritual delusion and religious fanaticism. I've seen it happen. The mystical experiences I've had always come as surprises; they have occurred during seasons when I was longing for and seeking God. The yearning heart of the psalmist is the soul of the mystic.

> As a deer longs for the flowing streams,
>> so my soul longs for you, O God.
> My soul thirsts for God,
>> for the living God.
> When shall I come and behold
>> the face of God? (Ps 42:1-2)

God promises, "When you search for me, you will find me; if you seek me with all your heart" (Jer 29:13). Seek God, not an experience. Be open to mystical experiences, but don't chase after them. Instead of focusing on mystical experiences, focus on spiritual formation. Through practices like disciplined Scripture reading, liturgical prayer, formative prayer, listening prayer, contemplative prayer, spiritual reading, and spiritual direction, we form our soul in healthy ways and increase our capacity to experience God. The heart, the spiritual organ for experiencing God, can be dull and insensitive or tender and alert. Through wise spiritual practices we keep our hearts healthy and capable of experiencing God.

Christians should regard mystical experiences as normative and even expect them, but they cannot be scheduled. To go on a spiritual retreat and say, "I'm going to have a mystical experience this weekend" almost always ends in disappointment. Seek God and let God's timing surprise you. And don't expect the mystical experiences of others to be your experience. We can read about the "showings" of Julian of Norwich or the stigmata of Saint Francis, but those were their mystical experiences, not ours. I find it beautiful that God reveals himself to each individual in unique ways. It's been said that no two mystics are alike—which is essentially the same thing as saying no two people are exactly alike. The infinite God who is our loving Father/Mother, though consistent, relates to every child in a special and inimitable way. This unique intimacy is hinted at in the book of Revelation when Jesus says he will give us "a new name that no one knows except the one who receives it" (Rev 2:17).

My final offer of advice to would-be mystics is to submit all mystical experiences to the test of time and tradition. If you've had a mystical experience, don't be too quick to talk about it. Give it some time. When Paul alludes to an experience of being caught up to heaven, he does so in the third person and fourteen years after the event (2 Cor 12:1-4). A supposed mystical experience that was nothing more than a flight of fancy will fade into the mists of time, but a real encounter with God is as everlasting as a diamond. Along with the test of time Christian mystical experiences should fit within the generous boundaries of Christian tradition. I would be highly suspicious of a mystical experience that seemed in conflict with Christian tradition as set forth in Scripture, creed, and historic orthodoxy. Paul had to remind the overly charismatic Corinthians of this when he tells them what should be obvious: "That no one speaking by the Spirit of God ever says 'Let Jesus be cursed!'" (1 Cor 12:3). Time and tradition can almost always faithfully adjudicate the veracity of a mystical experience.

The Christian of the future will be a mystic or nothing at all, said Karl Rahner fifty years ago. And now the future is here. Forty years ago, I read a book titled *Knowing God*, but as I look back these many years later, I realize that *Knowing God* isn't actually about knowing God but knowing doctrines *about* God—a presentation of Reformed systematic theology. I'm all for theology (though some theologies are better than others), but no matter how pristine our theological knowledge of God may be, it is not a substitute for actually *experiencing* God. The future age Rahner prophesied about is embodied by young people. And I know from my own experience of speaking to young people that most of them are not inherently interested in learning abstract theology, but nearly all of them are interested in the possibility of experiencing God. If Christianity is essentially about learning doctrines about God and adhering to behavioral codes, most of these young people will not remain Christian into their twenties. But if Christianity is essentially about *experiencing* the living God who is Father, Son, and Holy Spirit, these young people can be led into a holy mystery that will last a lifetime. The mystical Christianity I am advocating is the wardrobe that leads to the real-life Narnia.

◆   ◆   ◆

THE SYCAMORE'S PRAYERS

The enormous sycamore is older than internal
          combustion
Quieter too
I call it my sycamore tree
Which is funny
Because it more rightly calls me its human being
I've seen it get sick and I've seen it get well
It's a tough old tree
Once in an ice storm it impaled the ground with a spear
Zeus could not have done it better
It's not a tree to be trifled with
It watched Missouri hunt deer
Before there were houses here
Now it watches me
Read and write books
(The Missouri were more interesting)
For two decades it's stood guard
While I thought and thought and thought
And found a better way to think about God
And the tree thinks
I'm not as daft as when we first met
We hung a porch swing from its mightiest bough
(Sycamore doesn't mind)
It's my favorite place to pray
I think my prayers helped heal it once
And the sycamore's prayers have healed me
More than once

10

THE GRACE OF
SECOND NAIVETÉ

But someday you will be old enough
to start reading fairy tales again.

C. S. LEWIS, DEDICATION TO LUCY BARFIELD,
THE LION, THE WITCH AND THE WARDROBE

Twentieth-century French philosopher Paul Ricoeur coined the term *second naiveté* to express the possibility of a return to innocence after having once passed through the purging flames of critical thought. Ricoeur understood that with certain texts, especially religious texts, the meaning was not exhausted with a critical reading; beyond that remained the possibility for further meaning. At some point, the text can be reapproached and read with a second innocence or a new naiveté.

This phenomenon resonates with many Christians who have gone through some form of deconstruction or critical rethinking of their faith and joyfully discovered a revitalized faith on the other side. Healthy deconstruction is not an end in itself but a necessary, if messy, stage on the way to something better. Second naiveté is a grace given and a hopeful alternative to endless deconstruction. Drawing upon Ricoeur, Walter Brueggemann points out that "each of God's children is in transit along with the flow of orientation, disorientation, and reorientation."[1] We are not seeking a permanent disorientation of faith but a new reorientation within faith. This is what is given through the grace of second naiveté.

When we apply the grace of second naiveté to how we read the Bible, we can think of three stages: literal reading, analytical reading, and mystical reading. As children, we read the Bible in simplicity; we read it on a literal level. And there's nothing wrong with this. If some can remain untroubled with a literal reading of the Bible—a literal six-day creation, a literal Adam and Eve with a literal talking snake, Jonah in the belly of a literal whale, and so on—I'm not here to dissuade them of it. It's not my job to create trouble or force deconstruction on someone else. But in our post-Enlightenment world, most readers of the Bible eventually have no choice but to abandon a literal reading. So we learn about creation myths and the plethora of flood stories in the ancient world. We learn what a literary analysis reveals about the construction of the Bible. We learn about the documentary hypothesis and the possibility of a Q source informing the Synoptic Gospels. And we learn how to subject both Testaments to a historical-critical reading. For many of us, this is a necessary journey. And I find it fascinating. An analytical reading of the Bible has never imperiled my faith. But neither do I want to stay there forever. An analytical reading of the Bible should lead us beyond a literal reading into spiritual or mystical reading. So, for example, once I've deconstructed a literal reading of Genesis or Joshua, I can return to these books and read them on a much deeper level, no longer troubled by scientific contradictions or supposed divine violence. I know how to read the Hebrew conquest narratives analytically, applying the tools of modern scholarship, which solves some of the problems, but that reading is eventually exhausted. If we reach the point where we read the Bible *solely* through the historical-critical lens, it eventually ceases to be the sacred and living Word of God. It no longer has the capacity to enchant and inspire.

Again, I don't object to an analytical reading of the Bible, but I don't want to read it that way forever. And unless someone is a professional textual scholar, I doubt that they *would* read the Bible this way forever; eventually they reach the place where there are no more new readings—the text is exhausted, dead, and no longer meaningful.

An analytical reading of the Bible is not an end in itself but a bridge that crosses the chasm from the finite world of biblical literalism to the infinite world of biblical mysticism. One of the problems with both a literal reading and an analytical reading of the Bible is that both tend to limit the text to one meaning, thus reducing its capacity for ongoing revelation.

Years ago I heard a sermon in which the preacher calculated how much rain it would take per hour to cover Mount Everest in forty days. (The answer is a rather fantastical 362 inches per hour!) Applying a scientific method to a literal reading of Noah's flood is, among other things, an enormous exercise in missing the point. The Noah story is about the problem of escalating human violence, not meteorological phenomenon. But it's perhaps only slightly less pointless than doing nothing more with the story than engaging in a literary analysis of Genesis 6–8 as compared with the *Epic of Gilgamesh*. One is simplistic, the other is scholarly, but both are dead-end readings.

A mystical reading, though, has the potential for endless unfoldings of ongoing revelation. And lest you think this is some novel or liberal way of reading the Bible, this is the primary way that the Bible was read and interpreted in the apostolic and patristic periods. We see this in 1 Peter, where the Noah story is creatively used as a picture of baptism (see 1 Pet 3:20-21). An even better example of the kind of playful creativity that can arise in a mystical reading of the Bible is what Paul does when he tells the Corinthians that the Israelites in the wilderness "drank from the spiritual rock that followed them, and the rock was Christ" (1 Cor 10:4). What is Paul talking about? In Exodus 17, at the beginning of their forty-year journey through the wilderness, Moses brings forth water from a rock at Horeb. Later, in Numbers 20, the story is repeated with a slight change. Paul playfully imagines the two stories about a rock that miraculously gives water to Israel in the wilderness and in essence says, "That rock shows up twice in the Bible because it was following Israel through the wilderness. And guess what, that rock was Christ!" Does this mean Paul thought that Christ was *literally* a water-spewing rock crawling through the desert following the Israelites? Of course not. Paul is working creatively with the text, transcending "authorial intent" and giving new meaning to the ancient text. Commenting on Paul's mystical and allegorical reading of the rock in the wilderness, David Bentley Hart says:

> As should be obvious, Paul frequently allegorizes Hebrew scripture; the "spiritual reading" of scripture typical of the Church Fathers of the early centuries was not their invention, nor just something borrowed from pagan culture, but was already a widely accepted hermeneutical practice among Jewish scholars. So it is not anachronistic to read Paul here saying that the stories he is repeating are not accurate historical accounts of actual events, but allegorical tales composed for the edification of readers.[2]

COMING FULL CIRCLE

I long ago left behind a literal reading of the Bible. But now, at least to a certain extent, I find myself leaving behind an analytical reading of the Bible as well. So today, if I'm reading the Bible in the morning as part of my daily spiritual exercises and I read about the walls of Jericho falling down, I don't muse upon the fact that archaeological evidence does not support this. I know this fact, but now that I know it, I can set it aside and allow the inspired storyteller to tell the story. Because, although I know what biblical archaeology says about this story, I also know there are walls that need to fall and that the people of God need to march around these walls believing they will fall. I also know there are armies that need to be drowned in a sea and giants that need to be slain with a slingshot. The Bible wants to carry me beyond the constricting totalism of empire and toward the faith-imagined possibilities of the kingdom of God.

Can walls of hatred come tumbling down? Can injustice be hurled into the sea? Can the Goliath of racism be overcome? Yes! And one of the reasons I know of these possibilities is that every morning when I sit with my Bible I enter a world where these things happen all the time.

A second-naiveté reading of the Bible is not going back, it's not amnesia, it's not willful ignorance but a new appreciation for the divine genius at work in these inspired stories. We allow the text the freedom of the storyteller and allow ourselves to be enchanted by the story without having to constantly raise an empiricist "yeah, but." We are once again capable of being surprised by the Bible. If we don't have to forever read Joshua as a historical account of genocide, how might the story of liberated slaves successfully building a new society against overwhelming odds speak to us? We can return to a childlike innocence as we inhabit the stories of Scripture because we are, after all, children. When it comes to the knowledge of God, how can any of us claim to be anything more than kindergarteners? Yes, we are children—children of God. And like all children, we need the right stories to shape and inspire our imaginations.

Now in his eighties, esteemed German Catholic theologian and New Testament scholar Gerhard Lohfink describes how he has returned to a second-naïveté way of reading the Bible. Lohfink acknowledges that for a theologian, an analytical approach to Scripture is a requisite stage, but in his practice it has not been the final stage:

> Every theologian has to go through that phase. At any rate, I went through it, and I thoroughly enjoyed it. But now I want to read my Bible quite simply again. I carry the burden of scholarship with me in my backpack. It is necessary, and we have to bring it along with us, because it helps us to understand the text in its final form. And yet in the end I want to be carried forward by the text itself and its fascination. I rejoice in it. I am frightened by its claim. I allow myself to be consoled by it. I live in it like a child whose mother tells it a story at bedtime.[3]

As children, some form of literalism may be the only way of understanding the Bible. But as we progress into adulthood, biblical literalism increasingly belongs to the childish things that need to be put away for the sake of maturity. And then, to some extent, the process of subjecting the Bible to the rigors of modern analysis begins. But that should not be the end of the journey. The goal is to continue to grow and hopefully become, as C. S. Lewis said, "old enough to start reading fairy tales again."[4]

I don't mean that the Bible *is* a fairytale but that there is a holy and mature way of reading the Bible that is akin to how we read fairytales. If we read a story about a snake talking to Eve, we can accept it as we accept a wolf talking to Little Red Riding Hood. We don't let the fantastic elements prevent us from hearing the story, because it's the story that matters. To be clear, I don't treat all the stories in the Bible as allegorical. For example, I hold the resurrection of Jesus Christ to be a historical event. Though the precise nature of the resurrection may lie beyond our understanding, I believe it happened. I believe it because the living Christ has been revealed to me and because of the witness and creedal confession of the church. But we can, as we must, read much of the Old Testament as allegorical and still be as solidly orthodox as the church fathers.

When I first came to believe in Jesus in my teens, the Bible was a new book to me because I had not yet read it. Over the next thirty years, I devoured the Bible, reading it through several times a year. I read it simply, without assistance from serious scholarship. My goal was to ingest and inhabit the text—and I did. Much later, when I went through my water-to-wine theological renovation beginning in 2004, I read countless works of biblical scholarship written by trained academics, and I benefitted enormously from this. It made the Bible new to me again. During that time, I repeatedly told my church I had new eyes, and with my new eyes, the Bible had become a new book. But today I have deliberately returned to a simpler reading of the Bible, and for the third time, it has become a new book. I say I've returned, but it's not really that. The knowledge I gained from years of immersion in biblical scholarship is still with me, and I can draw upon it whenever I like. But for the most part, I now want to read the Bible like I did when I was sixteen.

Interestingly, the biblical scholars who have instructed me most encourage this kind of reading. In the end, the point of biblical scholarship is not to serve the academy but to serve a spiritual reading of the Bible. Lately, in my morning Bible reading, I've been using the King James Bible as a way of reminding myself how I want to read the Bible these days. I've read the modern and more accurate English translations for decades, and that knowledge operates in the background as I read, but the King James translation helps me to settle into a more poetic, more mythical, more mystical reading of the Bible. Verily, verily, it's the grace of second naiveté.

The Bible contains a lot of information, but the true purpose of the Bible is not to be an encyclopedia of *God facts*; rather it is to be a portal for engagement with God. This means that Scripture and prayer should go hand in hand. If all we do is *read* the Bible, we've not yet understood the spiritual purpose of our sacred text. Better than reading the Bible is *praying* the Bible, and this is where liturgy can be so helpful in spiritual formation. At its best, liturgy is the artistic and theological combination of Scripture and prayer. When we *read* the Bible, we place information in our head—and this has value. But when we *pray* the Bible, our heart engages with God—and this is far more valuable. This is why I deeply appreciate the traditions that in worship chant or sing the Scriptures. This practice helps remind worshipers that our engagement with Scripture is not primarily cerebral or academic but spiritual and religious. In attempting to speak of the divine, prose has its limits and eventually must yield to the more elevated language of poetry. There's a reason why so much of the Bible is in poetic form. Just as there is a reason why most of the Hebrew prophets were first of all poets. The poetic and prophetic are related. The great American poet Walt Whitman understood this:

> After the seas are all cross'd, (as they seem already cross'd,)
>
> After the great captains and engineers have accomplish'd their work,
>
> After the noble inventors, after the scientists, the chemist, the geologist, ethnologist,
>
> Finally shall come the poet worthy that name,
>
> The true son of God shall come singing his songs.[5]

A NONINTERVENTIONIST GOD?

The grace of second naiveté (or a return to innocence or recovered simplicity or a remythologized faith or whatever we may call what I'm attempting to describe) does not just influence our engagement with Scripture but our entire life of faith—it's the way back to Narnia. By Narnia, I mean that place of magic and adventure where Aslan (Christ) is, if not regularly, then periodically glimpsed and encountered. Narnia is the place where Aslan is on the move, where Aslan intervenes. In Narnia, we are saved only because Aslan intervenes. But for some, intervention is *verboten*. It's becoming increasingly common to hear those who have gone through some form of theological deconstruction say, "I no longer believe in an interventionist God." But this strikes me as little more than functional atheism. Are we back to the absent clockmaker God of the eighteenth-century deists? Who needs a noninterventionist God? What good is that God? If God doesn't intervene, then we must all save ourselves, which is to say we are all lost. A God who does not intervene is not the God of the Bible, not the God of love, and not the Father in heaven that Jesus talked about. If others no longer believe in an interventionist God, I resolutely do.

I recognize that fundamentalist Christianity—especially of the Pentecostal and charismatic variety—can be guilty of the theological error of turning God into a cosmic vending machine: insert the proper faith coins and out pops a miracle. In this system if you're sick, you use your faith to get healed, and if you don't get healed, it's because you don't have enough faith. It's a theological system where cruelty is heaped upon misfortune. So I certainly understand the need to deconstruct that kind of misconception of God. Transactional certitude has nothing to do with real faith. But to leap from there to "I no longer believe in an interventionist God" is an overreaction of the worst kind. It's just replacing one mistaken certitude with another.

Perhaps the most consistent picture of God given to us in Scripture is that of a deliberately intervening God. To say we cannot control the intervention of God is one thing, but to say that God does not intervene is something else altogether. Granted, it seems as though God doesn't intervene in our suffering near as often as we would like. Indeed, the highest expression of faith may be to continue to believe in God amid unjust suffering. This is the remarkable faith of Job. Commenting on Job's unrequited faith amid unjust suffering, Gustavo Gutiérrez writes,

> Can human beings have a disinterested faith in God—that is, can they believe in God without looking for rewards and fearing punishments? Even more specifically: Are human beings capable, in the midst of unjust suffering, of continuing to assert their faith in God and speak of God without expecting a return? Satan, and with him all those who have a barter conception of religion, deny the possibility. The author [of Job], on the contrary, believes it to be possible, although he undoubtedly knew the difficulty that human suffering, one's own and that of others, raises against authentic faith in God. Job, whom he makes the vehicle of his own experiences, will be his spokesman.[6]

Job on the ash heap of suffering reaches the pinnacle of faith when he declares, "Though He slay me, yet will I trust Him" (Job 13:15 NKJV). Nevertheless, in the end, God *did* intervene in Job's story, though not necessarily in the way Job had hoped.

Despite the reality of unjust suffering, I believe in an interventionist God. A God who intervened with creation. (What could be more intervening than that?) A God who intervened in the history of Israel and through the ministry of the prophets. A God who intervened decisively when the Logos was made flesh. The incarnation is the intervention that saves the world. When everything is on fire, my greatest comfort is the assurance that the world will be saved. God did not send his Son into the world to condemn the world but to save the world. Yes, the world will be saved by the intervention of God.

Nevertheless, prayers go unanswered, children die of cancer, and even the most faith-filled suffer "the slings and arrows of outrageous fortune."[7] God intervenes, but from our vantage point not nearly as often as we would like. It does create the temptation to fling our hands up in despair and say, "I no longer believe in an interventionist God." I understand this impulse, but I think it is mostly an attempt to seal ourselves off from potential disappointment. We give up praying lest we be disappointed, or we pray such safe prayers that we no longer run the risk of being disappointed. But if we are to have any hope for a life of vibrant faith, we have to run the risk of disappointment. Faith by its very nature is a risky venture. So I choose the risk of disappointment. I do this because it is my experience that God can help me bear disappointment, but if I quit engaging with God by ceasing to implore divine intervention in our world and in my life for fear of disappointment, my soul begins to waste away. I don't want to live in a world where God seems absent just because I don't want to risk disappointment.

I actually believe—though I cannot prove it—that God is in a *constant state of intervention* in the world. I hold to the seemingly outrageous idea that God is never *not* intervening in the world! God is love, and God is always loving the world. God's intervention is God's love. God's intervening love may rarely (if ever) be coercive and controlling, but the intervention of love is there nevertheless. What God's loving, though noncoercive, intervention looks like exactly is hard to tell, but I suspect that has more to do with our own spiritual blindness than with any imagined absence or ambivalence on God's part. I would even dare to suggest that the

day may come when we will look back and see that God's engagement with our life was one of constant intervening love. The
things that could have happened but didn't, unanticipated moments of quiet joy, simple acts of kindness given and received,
friendships that came to be, the strength to go on when we were
sure our strength was gone: these and a million other unrecog-
nized graces are what make life livable. And might these graces
flow from God's constant intervening love? I choose to believe so.

So, today I pray and read my Bible with new but hard-won simplicity. I expect the intervention of God, though I don't put too fine
of a point on what that might look like. I believe that the God who
parted the Red Sea will make a way where there seems to be none.
I believe that the God who was with the Hebrew children in the
fiery furnace will be with me when things get hot. I believe the God
who came to the disciples walking on the water will come to me
when I'm in stormy seas. And I believe the God who raised Jesus
Christ from the dead will, in the end, save us all from the final dissolution of death. This is the simple faith that sustains me in the
grace of second naiveté.

If the grace of second naiveté is the way back to Narnia, and I
believe it is, for I've made that journey myself, I don't want this
chapter to be viewed as prescriptive or how it's done—at least not
too much. Perhaps it's enough to be alerted that such a thing is
possible and thus hold on to hope. C. S. Lewis's wise professor in
The Lion, the Witch and the Wardrobe has something insightful to
say about this,

> Yes, of course you'll get back to Narnia someday. Once a King
> in Narnia, always a King in Narnia. But don't go trying to use
> the same route twice. Indeed, don't *try* to get there at all. It'll
> happen when you're not looking for it.[8]

11

THE HOUSE
OF LOVE

They say in your father's house, there's many mansions

Each one of them got a fireproof floor

BOB DYLAN, "SWEETHEART LIKE YOU"

I n 1425, **Andrei Rublev,** a Russian monk and iconographer,
created what would become one of the most famous icons in
history: *The Hospitality of Abraham*, more commonly known as
The Trinity. On one level, it's a depiction of the three angels who
dined with Abraham at the oaks of Mamre (see Gen 18). But on a
deeper level, it is an iconic representation of the Holy Trinity.
Rublev painted the icon during a time of political turmoil in
Russia; he wanted meditation on the icon to help his fellow monks
keep their souls at peace by fixing their hearts on God. In the icon,
the Trinity is seated at a four-sided table with the side nearest the

viewer left vacant. It's an invitation for the viewer to join the Trinity in their fellowship of divine love. In his meditation on icons, Henri Nouwen describes Rublev's *Trinity* as the "House of Love":

> To live in the world without belonging to the world summarizes the essence of the spiritual life. The spiritual life keeps us aware that our true house is not the house of fear, in which the powers of hatred and violence rule, but the house of love, where God resides. Hardly a day passes in our lives without our experience of inner or outer fears, anxieties, apprehensions, and preoccupations. These dark powers have pervaded every part of our world to such a degree that we can never fully escape them. Still it is possible not to belong to these powers, not to build our dwelling place among them, but to choose the house of love as our home. This choice is made not just once and for all but by living a spiritual life, praying at all times and thus breathing God's breath. Through the spiritual life we gradually move from the house of fear to the house of love.[1]

Today, everything seems to be on fire because the fallen world we live in is marred by fear, hatred, and violence. We see it in fearmongering politics that appeal to all that is worst in us; we see it in the ugly persistence of America's four centuries of white supremacist racism; we see it in the malignant gun culture and gun violence that terrorizes our land from Columbine to Sandy Hook to Everywhere, USA; and we see it in expressions of American Christianity that willingly embrace political policies that are unapologetically cruel and unkind. In a time when everything is on fire with fear, hatred, and violence, the temptation is to fear the fear, hate the hate, and react with violence to the violence. It's easy to be seduced into thinking that *our* fear is warranted, *our* hate is righteous, and *our* violence is justified. This is the devil handing out cans of gasoline to the citizens of a city on fire.

But as Henri Nouwen points out, the essence of the spiritual life is to live in a fallen world without belonging to it. To be holy is not so much to be "good" in a moralistic sense but to be *other*. Conservatives shout "line up on the right!" while progressives shout "line up on the left!" Meanwhile, Jesus calls us to something other, something altogether different, something that cannot be plotted on the unimaginative left-right grid. The goal of the spiritual life is to live into that holy and transcendent *other* way of being. The pathologies that have sickened our society are often bred in the house of fear. The master of the house of fear is a cruel torturer. As the apostle John says, "fear hath torment" (1 Jn 4:18 KJV). The occupants in the torturer's house of fear often become cruel people. And it really doesn't matter if the cruelty comes in the form of left-leaning or right-leaning ideology. In the house of fear, identity politics tends to push the adherents to the cruel edges. The solution is not moderation but a new residence.

Through a spiritual life—a grace-empowered life that transcends the world as it is—we gradually change our residence from the cruel house of fear to the peaceable house of love. It doesn't happen all at once. It's not as simple as walking an aisle or praying a sinner's prayer. It takes more than just making up your mind to be more loving. It's not easy, but it is possible. To move from the house of fear to the house of love is the purpose of spiritual formation and the goal of contemplative prayer. The reason we seek to be properly formed through spiritual practices is so we can eventually take up permanent residence in the house of love. When everything is on fire, our refuge is the house of love—a house that is impermeable to the flames of fear, hatred, and violence. This doesn't mean that we are not affected by the fires raging in our society like everyone else, but it does mean that it's possible for our inner self to remain untouched by the flames of hell.

The apostle Paul says, "So we do not lose heart. Even though our outer nature is wasting away, our inner nature is being renewed day by day" (1 Cor 4:16). Though we are grieved at the hellish happenings in our society, we're not destroyed by them. For those who have learned how to live in the house of love, there is inner peace. This is what Rublev was trying to communicate to his brothers in the tumultuous fifteenth century with his icon, and it's what I'm trying to communicate to my sisters and brothers in a tumultuous twenty-first century with this book.

Wars big and small, verbal and martial constantly break out in the house of fear. In the house of fear, the illusion of scarcity dominates. There's never enough in the house of fear, so its inhabitants think they have to fight for their share. In the house of fear, we cannot welcome the stranger or care for the poor because there may not be enough for us. The satan—as the instigator of accusation and the inciter of anxiety—rules in this diabolical house. It's a dysfunctional household where every other occupant is viewed as a potential rival, a competitor who must be bested, a contestant to be conquered. In this dreadful house, friendships are mostly calculated alliances; people are a disposable means to a selfish end. This is the bleak summation of much of world history. This is what lurks behind the grim story of the European conquest and colonization of the Americas. The native peoples didn't meet a new neighbor; they were invaded by conquistadors. Columbus discovered the new world like that asteroid discovered the dinosaurs. Armed with "germs, guns, and steel" the invaders from the house of fear brought death to two continents.[2] It was the Cain and Abel story retold on a hemispheric scale. Yes, much of what we call world history is just the diary of events from the house of fear.

Humanity's house of fear is home to all our worst maladies. It's where we are schooled in blame and require the sacrifice of a scapegoat. It's the house of rage, the house of war, the house of death. It is, in fact, hell. Hell here and now, hell by and by, hell as long as we exile ourselves from the house of love. But—it's all a lie! The house of fear is a false construct built in pernicious deception by the father of lies. The house of fear exists only because its inhabitants don't yet know the single greatest truth of our existence: *God is love.* The universe is not benign, but God is love. Cruel vagaries abound, but God is love. Harms are hidden among us, but God is love. An awareness of God's love is the secret to facing the world as it is and still abiding in peace.

It's true that the universe is not benign—twenty-four thousand people are killed by lightning every year—but God is love, and God loves every one of them. We can't deny that cruel vagaries abound, babies get brain cancer and brides die on their wedding day, but God is love and will redeem their stories. We know that harms are hidden among us, a fragment of genetic material can unleash a deadly global pandemic, but God is love, and love alone will have the last word. I'm not naive. Every moment of existence, we are at risk. We are never perfectly safe, but we are always perfectly loved. And it is perfect love that casts out all fear (1 Jn 4:18). We don't have to stay a frightened and miserable hostage in the house of fear; the Holy Trinity invites us to take up residence in their house of eternal love. Jesus says,

> Do not let your hearts be troubled. Believe in God, believe also in me. In my Father's house there are many dwelling places. If it were not so, would I have told that I go to prepare a place for you? And if I go and prepare a place for you, I will come again and will take you to myself, so that where I am, there you may be also. (Jn 14:1-3)

BELIEVE IN GOD!

When everything is on fire, can we hear Jesus say to us, "Do not let your hearts be troubled. Believe in God"? When we're distressed by dark clouds pouring calamity upon us, is it false comfort or sage wisdom to take shelter in God? I choose to believe it is the latter because Jesus says so. Perhaps the primary reason I believe in God is because Jesus does. I've heard the cynical say, "God is a crutch." For me, God is much more than a crutch. God is my rock of safety, a high tower, a mighty fortress, a bulwark never failing, a shelter from the storm. So when Jesus tells my troubled heart to believe in God, I do!

But Jesus also says, "Believe in me." *God* (from the German *Got*) is an abstract sign, a concept, an empty vessel we can pour our ideas into. For most Western people, *God* is the amalgamation of all the philosophical *omnis*—omniscient, omnipotent, omnipresent, omni-everything. With this approach to understanding God, we merely embrace our own ideas, preferences, prejudices, and fears magnified to the omni-degree. But a Christian understanding of God is *entirely* informed by Jesus. He defines God, not the philosophical *omnis*. We don't know God according to philosophical categories but by the revelation of Jesus Christ. Jesus says, "No one knows the Father except the Son and anyone to whom the Son chooses to reveal him" (Mt 11:27).

The whole point of confessing the deity of Christ is to know what God is like. We must not make the mistake of saying, "I already know what God is like, and now I know that Jesus is that." No! That's backward. We *don't* know what God is like! Jesus alone knows the Father and reveals the Father. The whole point of confessing the deity of Christ is to know what God is like. God is like Jesus! Every other idea about God—no matter where it comes from—must bow to the revelation of God as seen in Jesus. The Bible is not the perfect revelation of God; Jesus is. What the Bible does best is to faithfully point us to Jesus as the revelation of God. To say "I believe in God" is often an enormous empty signifier because *God* can be an endlessly malleable concept. We believe in God *ambiguously* and *vaguely*, mostly as a philosophical concept and psychological projection. But when we believe in Jesus as the perfect revelation of God, we begin to encounter God in *specificity* and *particularity*. The writer of Hebrews is quite explicit about this when he says that Jesus is "the exact imprint of God's very being" (Heb 1:3).

This audacious claim has led some to stumble at the scandal of particularity. More than a few modern minds are offended at the idea that the Logos of God became *particular* flesh—in a *particular* place, at a *particular* moment in history. The idea that God entered history and joined the human race uniquely through Jesus of Nazareth with all his particularities offends the more pantheistic and perhaps more palatable idea that God is all things. But this offense, if it is an offense, is an inherent aspect of orthodox Christianity. "We proclaim Christ crucified, a stumbling block to Jews and foolishness to Gentiles" (1 Cor 1:23).

I've heard some from the outer edges of progressive Christianity blithely chirp, "Christ is everything." That's pious-sounding nonsense. Christ is not cancer cells, Christ is not nuclear bombs, Christ is not my cat, and Christ is not me. Christians confess that all things will be assumed into and healed by Christ, but this happens *through* the scandal of particularity, not apart from it. In his great treatise on the resurrection, the apostle Paul sets forth a sweeping eschatological vision that culminates with God being all and in all:

> For since death came through a human being, the resurrection of the dead has also come through a human being; for as all die in Adam, so all will be made alive in Christ. But each in his own order: Christ the firstfruits, then at his coming those who belong to Christ. Then comes the end, when he hands over the kingdom to God the Father, after he has destroyed every ruler and authority and power. For he must reign until he has put all enemies under his feet. The last enemy to be destroyed is death. For "God has put all

things in subjection under his feet." But when it says, "all things are put in subjection," it is plain that this does not include the one who put all things in subjection under him. When all things are subjected to him, then the Son himself will also be subjected to the one who put all things in subjection under him, *so that God may be all in all*. (1 Cor 15:21-28, emphasis added)

The glorious crescendo of Christian eschatology is the abolition of death and the arrival of a healed cosmos in which God is all in all. But this redemptive end is accomplished through the particularity of Christ. And I, for one, am not offended by this scandal of particularity. I'm particularly partial to Jesus Christ! In response to the eschatology set forth in the New Testament, I am *universal* in my robust hope that all creation will be redeemed, and I am *particular* in my confession that this redemption is accomplished in Christ. Our blessed hope is that the Father's house will finally subsume the entire cosmos—that the universe itself will become the house of love. But the particular good news in our present moment is that Jesus invites us to live in the house of love now.

When Jesus says, "In my Father's house there are many dwelling places," he is saying something like this: "In my Father's house of infinite love there is room for everyone—no one needs to be excluded." Our hope is that the house of fear will be abandoned, left vacant, and finally demolished. Because life in the house of fear is barely life at all. It's more like the horror of Edgar Allan Poe's *The Pit and the Pendulum*—the walls closing in, death drawing near, and no escape. But Jesus says he *is* the escape. When Philip asked Jesus about the way to the Father's house, Jesus said, "I am the way, and the truth, and the life" (Jn 14:6). When we follow the Jesus way, embrace the Jesus truth, and live the Jesus life, we are on the road to the Father's house, the house of love. And do I believe that some, drawn by the Holy Spirit, are on this holy way without yet knowing the name of the way? Absolutely. They are what Karl Rahner called "anonymous Christians."[3]

The reason I cannot be a cynic, the reason I refuse to despair, the reason I hold on to hope despite everything being on fire is that, along with the apostle Paul, I too am "convinced that neither death, nor life, nor angels, nor rulers, nor things present, nor things to come, nor powers, nor height, nor depth, nor anything else in all creation, will be able to separate us from the love of God in Christ Jesus our Lord" (Rom 8:38-39). And so I say it without embarrassment: everything is going to be all right. Or in the famous words of the English mystic Julian of Norwich, "It is true that sin is the cause of all this pain, but all will be well, and all will be well, and all manner of things will be well."[4] How can it be otherwise? If we are truly loved by God, everything is going to be all right. If we are truly loved by God, we can afford to trust instead of fight. If we are truly loved by God, we can abandon the house of fear. If we are truly loved by God, we can live in the house of love here and now. This is what I believe. And it's not a careless slide into easy believism but the spoils of a hard-won struggle for faith. Once faith has won the day, or at least gained a foothold, we are free to dream dreams.

THE DREAMS I DREAM

On the day of Pentecost, the apostle Peter began the first Christian sermon by drawing upon a text from the prophet Joel.

> In the last days it will be, God declares,
> that I will pour out my Spirit upon all flesh,
>   and your sons and your daughters shall prophesy,
>   and your young men shall see visions,
>   and your old men shall dream dreams. (Acts 2:17)

Joel says the outpouring of the Spirit results in dreams and visions. They're similar, but not exactly the same. Visions are prose and need a plan; dreams are poetry and need only be dreamed. Visions are still a little bit tethered to what we tend to think is possible; dreams are a portal to a world where all things are possible. Dreams are truly transcendental—we are free to dream of things that we have no idea how they could come to pass. I'm not talking about daydreams, pipedreams, idle dreams; I'm talking about Spirit-inspired dreams. As I have opened to the Spirit—the agent of all possibility—I've dreamed some dreams about a future church.

I dream of a church that is a house of love, a city of refuge, a shelter from the storm. The beleaguered souls in the house of fear desperately need a house of love. The accused, canceled, and set upon need a city of refuge. The weary and worn, exhausted from the constant strain of caustic culture wars, need shelter from the storm. This is precisely what the church is called to be. Sunday morning should be a weekly leave from the constant battle of life. The password in our churches is the exchange of peace: "The peace of Christ be with you." "And also with you."

I dream of a church that is a pioneer in the way of peace and never again a chaplain to the masters of war. The greatest infidelity of the church has been to serve the masters of war. In the hagiographic legend, Constantine, on the eve of the battle for the Milvian Bridge, saw a cross in the heavens with the words, "In this sign you shall conqueror." That was the beginning of killing in the name of the cross—a grotesque departure from the nonviolent peace tradition the church had held for three centuries. At the Milvian Bridge, a deal was made with the devil that eventually led to the two world wars in Europe where baptized Christians slaughtered one another by the millions in the name of their national allegiance. The future of the church is found in its primal past of renouncing war and waging peace.

I dream of a church that excels in contemplative practices and contemplative stances. Instead of culture-war Christians, we need contemplative Christians. The problem with the Christian left and the Christian right is that *Christian* gets reduced to adjective duty in service to the all-important ideological noun, and the last thing the world or the church needs is another reactionary left-right ideologue. Archbishop Lazar Puhalo says, "When religion collapses into an ideology it is no longer faith. Religion itself becomes lust when what you call love is motivated by hate."[5] Through the practices of contemplative prayer, we move out of the realm of reactive dualism. The ultimate goal of contemplative prayer is not detachment but a solid grounding in love.

I dream of a church that is at home in God's good world instead of huddled anxiously at the departure gate. The idea that the goal of the Christian life is to go to heaven in general, and rapture theology in particular, has done incalculable damage to how millions of believers think about the future. The Christian eschatological hope is not to go to heaven but to bring heaven to earth. The blessed hope is not that we're going but that Christ is coming. The closing scene in the book of Revelation is a picture of heaven and earth reunited in holy matrimony—a promise that is in the process of becoming. Jesus Christ as set forth in Scripture is the Savior of the world—not the Savior of parts of people for another world. Christians who are correctly taught what the Bible proclaims from Genesis to Revelation should of all people lead the way in caring for God's good earth.

I dream of a church in which faith and science are not at odds. In 1633, Galileo was found "vehemently suspect of heresy" for championing the Copernican theory of heliocentrism. Under threat of torture, Galileo was forced to recant. The Roman Catholic Church at the dawn of modernity thought that if the earth was not the center of the cosmos, then the Bible was proved wrong and the Christian faith would collapse. Of course, we know now that Copernicus and Galileo were correct and the Catholic Church was mistaken; the earth revolves around the sun and Christianity did not collapse. From this colossal embarrassment, the Catholic Church learned a valuable lesson and now celebrates scientific inquiry. Today, science classes in Catholic high schools in the United States spend more time studying evolution than the science classes in public high schools. It's time for evangelicals to learn the lesson that Catholics have learned. I regularly tell my church that I don't know of a single peer-reviewed scientific theory that is a threat to the Christian faith. All truth is God's truth, and in the end, scientists and theologians are seeking the same thing.

I dream of a church that is conservative because wisdom traditions are worth preserving. I have a deep respect for theological conservatism—not the faux conservatism of modern fundamentalism but the true conservatism that draws upon patristic tradition. Christianity is a received faith; we don't get to make it up. Christianity remains a living faith while it remains rooted in its ancient soil. Jesus said, "Every scribe who has been trained for the kingdom of heaven is like the master of a household who brings out of his treasure what is new and what is old" (Mt 13:52). The church is the custodian of treasures old and new.

I dream of a church that is progressive because the journey is ongoing. All that needs to be said in the ongoing conversation of Christian theology has not yet been said. In the Upper Room Discourse, Jesus told his disciples, "I still have many things to say to you, but you cannot bear them now. When the Spirit of truth comes, he will guide you into all the truth" (Jn 16:12-13). Conservatism alone will not enable the church to come into all the truth. David Bentley Hart points out that the members of the heretical Arian party were, when all is said and done, the theological conservatives of their time and place; the members of the Nicene party were the daring innovators. The former were traditionalists, and for that reason their language ultimately proved sterile; the latter were theological and metaphysical radicals, and as a consequence their language gave the tradition new and enduring life.[6]

I dream of a church that is a viable alternative to soulless secularism. Philosophical secularism is the modern idea that God is irrelevant for the organization of our lives and that there is nothing ontologically sacred. In secularism, the sacred is merely an artificial construct. But a world without the sacred is a world without a soul. The yearning for the sacred is part of what it means to be human—this yearning can be suppressed, but it cannot be extinguished. The church doesn't need to fight secularism; the church just needs to be an alternative to secularism. We need churches that are less practical and more sacramental.

I dream of a church in which my grandchildren's grand-children learn to love and follow Jesus. I'm playing the long game. I'm not just in this for myself. It's doubtful that my great-great-grandchildren will know my name (do you know the names of your great-great-grandparents?), but still I want to leave them a gift. So I give my life in service to the church because the church matters—it's how we pass on the pearl of great price to future generations. One way that we love our children and grandchildren is to love the good work of the church.

I dream that maybe we're still the early church. Selah. In the year of our Lord 9021, today's church will be regarded as the early church. Can we be content with a caretaker's role, or do we have to be the "omega generation"? We need to live with both an antici-pation of the imminent return of the Lord and with a suspicion that the parousia might be many millennia in the future.

I dream that the church of the distant future will kindly forgive our faults, for we too are people of our time. What are these faults? What are the errors we're blind to? I'm not sure. That's the point. It's hard to know what you don't know. It's hard to see what you can't see. We aren't a perfect church. We won't be a perfect church. We can't be a perfect church. For now, it will have to be enough to be a church struggling imperfectly to be faithful. And since grace is given to the humble, let us be humble.

I dream of a church in the distant future using technology I can't imagine, but still practicing sacraments I immediately recognize. Just as the church of the catacombs could not imagine the technologies we casually employ today, so we cannot imagine the technologies that will be available to the church of the twenty-fifth century. But the church of the catacombs would recognize baptism and Eucharist. These are the sacraments that bind us together across the ages.

These are some of the dreams I dream. Can you dream with me?

CONCLUSION

Every Bush Ablaze

> *We only live, only suspire*
> *Consumed by either fire or fire.*
>
> T. S. ELIOT, "FOUR QUARTETS"

No one looms larger in the story of the First Testament than Moses. Moses the deliverer, Moses the lawgiver, Moses the man who talks face-to-face with God, Moses the man who goes toe-to-toe with Pharaoh. But at midlife, Moses was a forgotten figure with a scandalous past; a former prince in Pharaoh's court, he was now a fugitive working for his father-in-law in the outback. Moses was a washed-up has-been. In his wilderness years, Moses is a picture of the multitudes of lonely people who lost their ideals thirty-five years before and now can only put a touch of a smile over a mask of pain. At this point, it seems that middle-aged

Moses has entered the slow decline toward the final dissolution. Of course, we know this is not the end of the story. Moses is about to enter the second half of life bursting with significance and brimming with miracles.

But in between Moses the pharaonic prince and Moses the deliverer of Israel are the forgotten years. The years of stripping away, the years when Moses is scoured by the desert. In Egypt, Moses was a child of Pharaoh. In the wilderness, Moses became a child of God. Moses couldn't become who he became by going straight from darling prince to heroic deliverer. He tried, but that ended with a body buried in the sand and a flight into the desert. Yet there the desert did its slow work of stripping Moses down so God could build him back up. The process will be repeated in Israel's forty years of wandering in the wilderness and reflected in Jesus' forty days of fasting in the wilderness. Whether forty years or forty days, the work of the wilderness is necessary.

What is it about deserts and mountains that attract mystics and monks? These wilderness places are quiet and uncluttered spaces that offer a broad expanse. It's the kind of landscape where the soul can slow down, get quiet, and eventually expand. Egypt, on the other hand, is an ambitious and driven 24/7 make-more-bricks competitive consumer culture. Though most will only ever slave away in the merciless brick kilns, a few will succeed, get rich, and claw their way to the top. But it comes at the cost of an undeveloped soul. The soul of a mystic is more likely to be formed in Death Valley than in Silicon Valley.

Moses had flunked out of the Egyptian top one percent and is now a nomadic shepherd herding a flock not his own. However, Moses doesn't know that he's in school—the "wilderness school of midlife disillusionment"—so that his soul can expand. Moses is beginning to grow. Moses is about to wake up. And the awakening came suddenly—if you call forty years sudden. He was keeping his father-in-law's flock near Mount Sinai in the most remote part of the wilderness when he noticed it: a bush on fire. A bush was burning and burning but wasn't burned up. The bush was on fire, that was obvious, but the bush remained verdant and alive. It was a wonder. Moses had never seen anything like this before:

> Then Moses said, "I must turn aside and look at this great sight and see why the bush is not burned up." When the LORD saw that he had turned aside to see, God called to him out of the bush, "Moses, Moses! . . . Remove the sandals from your feet, for the place on which you are standing is holy ground." (Ex 3:3-5)

All that Moses became and accomplished—delivering the Hebrew slaves, parting the Red Sea, delivering the Ten Commandments, leading Israel to the Promised Land—began with this mystical encounter. Moses notices a bush. It's on fire. It's on fire but not consumed. He turns aside to contemplate the sight, and he encounters the living God! Before the encounter is over, Moses learns God's mysterious and holy name: I am who I am. When Moses made space for contemplation, he encountered the divine. When Moses awakened to wonder, he met God personally. When Moses was enlightened, the first thing he learned was that he was on holy ground. He took off his shoes because that's what you do when you're on holy ground. Of course, if you were to see a miraculous burning bush like Moses did, you might know you are on holy ground. Well, I've seen the burning bush.

APPOINTMENT ON MOUNT SINAI

In 2006, I made an appointment with God. I had just completed twenty-five years of ministry and wanted to prepare for the next twenty-five. I asked God to meet me on the summit of Mount Sinai at sunrise on November 9, 2006. That date was the thirty-second anniversary of my teenage encounter with Jesus Christ—the event that determined the entire trajectory of my life.

After celebrating the twenty-fifth anniversary of our church, Peri and I flew to Tel Aviv and then onto Eilat by the Red Sea. The next morning, we walked across the border into Egypt where we met the guide and driver we had hired to take us to St. Catherine's monastery at the foot of Mount Sinai. Our guide was a young man named Mina, a charismatic Egyptian Orthodox Christian. Our driver was Ahmed, a local Bedouin. Because of the presence of Al-Qaeda in the Sinai, Mina and Ahmed insisted that we take a security guard with us, so we were joined by Muhammad from Cairo—a former policeman who carried an Uzi submachine gun under his jacket. The journey from Eilat to St. Catherine's through the Sinai wilderness in a Toyota Land Cruiser is one of the most memorable adventures of my life. Ahmed preferred to travel off-road on a route known only to Bedouins. The journey was both thrilling and tortuous—Mina and I both suffered from car sickness. Along the way, we stopped to explore a slot canyon and later to share a meal with Bedouins, experiencing their famed hospitality. While having dinner in the Bedouin tent, I learned that Mohammad and his wife had recently suffered the loss of a child. It was a poignant moment when this Muslim security guard opened his heart to me.

We arrived at the monastery long after dark. We were told that it would take four hours to hike to the 7,500-foot summit of Sinai, so after only a few hours of sleep, we were on the trail at 2 a.m. It turned out that it only took us two hours to reach the summit—meaning we had arrived two hours before the 6 a.m. sunrise. The temperature was right at freezing, and we only had light jackets. For two hours, we shivered in the dark awaiting sunrise. But it was worth it. The sunrise was stunning—hues of purple on the horizon with fog nestled in the valleys of the fierce landscape. There's a reason why the Bible calls Sinai the mountain of God. On the holy mountain, God and I kept our appointment; we talked about the future and what I should do with the next quarter of a century. Then Peri and I hiked back down the mountain and for the first time saw St. Catherine's Monastery by the light of day. Christian monks first began living here in the year 330. Today, it's the site of the oldest continual worship in the Christian world. Five times a day for almost seventeen centuries Christians have gathered to worship at this site.

St. Catherine's also houses the oldest continually operating library in the world. One of the Greek Orthodox monks gave us a tour of the monastery. We saw their church; the *Ashtiname,* a document granting protection to Christian monks and pilgrims, sealed with the handprint of Mohammad; the original *Christ Pantocrator,* the oldest icon in the world, and finally the monk led us to the courtyard of the monastery and showed us . . . *the burning bush!* Without irony, the monk simply told us this was the burning bush where Moses met God. It was a large, ordinary-looking, viny kind of bush. Technically, it's a *rubus sanctus* or holy bramble, a desert shrub known for its longevity.

But is it *the* burning bush? Of course, it is. The holy bramble in the courtyard of St. Catherine's Monastery is the burning bush just like the giant sycamore in my backyard is the burning bush. What makes the burning bush the burning bush is not the bush but the awakening of Moses or me or you. Elizabeth Barrett Browning says it better in poetry than I can in prose:

> Earth's crammed with heaven,
> And every common bush afire with God,
> But only he who sees takes off his shoes;
> The rest sit round and pluck blackberries.[1]

In a secular age when everything is on fire, we may ask, where is God? I understand the impulse and the nature of the question (as I think this book has shown), but the mystic may very well answer, where *isn't* God? Is everything on fire with that which threatens to consume the sacred, or is the deeper truth that everything is on fire with the glory of God? Certainly, our world seems aflame with destructive forces, but the wise poet knows that's not the whole story; she has seen beyond the veil and bears witness that earth is crammed with heaven and every common bush is afire with God. Every bush, every tree, every bird, every blade of grass, every grain of sand, and the very stars themselves are all on fire with the glory of God. But in our hurry to be or do something, we rush past it all and miss the love of God smiling through all things. This creates the poverty of soul that we often experience as boredom. We fail to notice the glory that is flashing all around us.

When Moses awakened to the glory, he removed his shoes. The burning bush there was indeed a miracle, but the miracle wasn't so much in the bush as it was in Moses. At midlife, after experiencing deep loss, Moses suddenly awakened to wonder and turned aside to behold the glory of God in a simple desert bush. And having turned aside, Moses finally glimpsed the shining beauty that is in all of creation.

The problem that plagues the sons and daughters of modernity is that we so rarely turn aside. We're always on our way somewhere else. We so rarely inhabit the moment fully. We're distracted, we're in a hurry, we rush about, we're anxious, we're angry, we're empty. This is Egypt, this is Babylon, this is America, this is a disenchanted age devoid of glory, this is a world set on fire from the lamp of a madman declaring the death of God. This is life made unlivable and God made unknowable. We need a desert, a wilderness, a Sinai where our soul can grow still and then expand. And we don't need Mina, Ahmed, and Muhammad to take us there—we can find our way to holy ground. A park, a library, a quiet room, an empty cathedral, a walk in the woods will do. It's possible to enter the mystical wilderness within. Learn to sit in some kind of wilderness until something catches fire.

Take off your shoes and begin to talk to God as if God is there, as if God is near, as if God hears, as if God cares—because it's all true.

If you *want* to find God, begin with believing. Believe God is there *before* you have any evidence of it. Seek God, speak to God, listen for God, and see what happens. Don't wait until you have incontrovertible evidence before you believe; dare to take a leap and believe before you have evidence. It's as we leap across whatever chasm has challenged our credulity that we soar into faith and land on holy ground. Holy ground—the place where the ordinary begins to blaze with the glory of God. It's not hard to believe when you're on holy ground because you hear the Holy One whisper: *I am who I am.*

The world's on fire, but there are different kinds of fire. There is the fire that Moses beheld in the burning bush—a fire of glory that blazes but does not consume. And there is the malevolent fire that consumes and destroys—the devouring fire of Gehenna. What can we do when everything is on fire with the flames of destruction? We can take shelter in the love of God. We can seek the grace of resilience found in prayer. We can hold on to the hope that this too shall pass. *And* we can remember that even a consuming fire is not all bad, for it can lead to the goodness of new life. We see this in nature. Fire is part of the life cycle of the great forests. Some pine trees produce serotinous cones that are glued shut with a strong resin, and the cone opens only when the resin is melted by fire. Other pine trees produce seeds in their cones that only germinate when exposed to fire. These kinds of trees are dependent on the destruction of a forest fire to reproduce. Resin-sealed cones and fire-activated seeds await the flames that will liberate them. For these trees, fire is not the end but the beginning.

Christianity may be like these fire-dependent trees. Sometimes we need some old things to burn down before we can have new growth. We don't always realize that some of what we cherish is just the wood, hay, and straw of dead religion that we would be better off without. It's clear that much of the church in Western Europe and North America is being consumed in the scorching flames of modernity, but this doesn't mean it's the end of the Christian forest. These flames can be a purging fire that will ultimately liberate the church from lifelessness and clear the way for a Spirit-infused newness.

> No one can lay any foundation other than the one that has been laid; that foundation is Jesus Christ. Now if anyone builds on the foundation with gold, silver, precious stones, wood, hay, straw—the work of each builder will become visible, for the Day will disclose it, because it will be revealed with *fire*, and the *fire* will test what sort of work each has done. (1 Cor 3:11-13, emphasis added)

Faith and a church built on the foundation of Christ will endure, but from time to time our faith and the church needs a consuming fire to purge the deadwood that has accumulated. "Our God is a consuming fire" (Heb 12:29). We are currently facing a day when the fires of judgment are disclosing the quality of our work. Christendom is mostly deadwood, and whether the church realizes it or not, the fires of secularism that spell the demise of Christendom are rendering us good service. Let the old wood of religious nationalism that propped up an empire be consumed in secular flames. Let the rotten straw of consumer Christianity perish in the furnace of late modernity. Amen.

The resin-sealed cones of the gospel of the kingdom and the fire-activated seeds of genuine faith will open and germinate when everything is on fire. We will come through the fire chastened and reduced, but with the possibility of new growth. There is no return to a medieval Christendom when the church strode across society like a Colossus. So be it. That was always a grotesque distortion of the kingdom of Christ—an incongruous conflation of faith and empire. It was a disastrous attempt to unite the cross and the sword into a single instrument. It was folly that first led to the madness of the crusades and finally led to millions of German Christians saluting the swastika. Yes, the Christendom of Western Europe is already mostly in ashes, and the North American version of Christendom will suffer a similar demise, despite the misguided dreams of the religious right. But lying dormant within the eternal kingdom of heaven are the resin-sealed cones and fire-activated seeds, and I'm eager to see what a fire-purged faith of the future will look like. Even if I don't live to see it, I find comfort in believing that my grandchildren and their generation will. What can we do when everything is on fire? We can rejoice that it's not the end.

APOKATASTASIS PARK

When Peri and I lead our pilgrim tours of the Holy Land, one of my favorite things is to take people to hell. Literally. It's a short walk from our hotel in Jerusalem. I'm talking about the Valley of Hinnom or Gehenna. It's located just below the southern walls of the Old City. In the Bronze Age, this valley was a Canaanite site of Molech worship—an abominable practice where children were sacrificed in the burning belly of a bronze idol with the head of a bull. In the seventh century BC, King Josiah defiled this site "which is in the Valley of Ben-hinnom, so that no one would make a son or daughter pass through fire as an offering to Molech" (2 Kings 23:10). The valley then became the city dump for Jerusalem—a place of rotting refuse full of maggots and constantly burning fires.

For the sixth-century Hebrew prophets Isaiah and Jeremiah, and later for Jesus, Gehenna was used as the metaphorical image of total destruction or, as the King James Bible translates Gehenna, *hell*. It's the horrible place where, as Isaiah and Jesus say, "their worm never dies, and the fire is never quenched" (Mk 9:48). Jeremiah and Jesus both warned Jerusalem that if they didn't walk in the way of justice and peace, the whole city would end up a smoldering, maggot-infested Gehenna. This is hell. And Jerusalem has gone to hell twice, first in 587 BC and again in AD 70. This is the literal hell I take our pilgrims to. Except that today, it is Gey Ben Hinnom Park. A lovely green expanse with lawns, trees, fountains, couples walking hand in hand, and the occasional evening concert. I always enjoy taking pilgrims there and saying, "Welcome to hell." And then I point to the sign that says, "No Fires Allowed in the Park." It's a beautiful lesson in the hope of ultimate reconciliation.

If I could rename the Gey Ben Hinnom Park, I would call it Apo-katastasis Park—the park of the restoration of all things. What can we do when everything is on fire? We can remember that even the fires of hell are not the end of the story. I have living proof that even Gehenna can become a garden, that even hell can become a park—a garden park where no fires are allowed and the fountains are never quenched.

Demagogues may come and go, but Jesus is Lord. Empires will rise and fall, but the kingdom of Christ endures. Woes will surely ebb and flow, but there is stability in the peace of Christ. No matter what happens, I believe in Jesus Christ, and because of Christ, I can smile at the future. The world will be saved because Jesus is the Savior of the world. You can call this circular reasoning or a logical fallacy, but I call it the gospel. Because it is God who saves, in the end the world cannot be anything other than saved. Today's fiery Gehenna is the future's Apokatastasis Park. My resolute hope is for the final transfiguration of this world.

When Jesus prayed on Mount Tabor, he was transfigured—his face shone like the sun and his clothing became dazzling white. The divinity within was now shining without. He was still Jesus of Nazareth with the visage of a Galilean Jew, but now Peter, James, and John saw him in the fullness of his glory—the glory of divine transfiguration. And in the transfiguration of Christ, I find my hope for the world. I believe that what was seen in the transfiguration of

Christ will become the reality of this good but fallen creation. I confess that this beloved world will finally be redeemed from the bondage of decay and shine like the sun. I am persuaded by the witness of the Holy Spirit that someday everything will be on fire with the divine glory of God. This is my hope. I invite you to embrace this hope. I invite you to believe in God.

♦   ♦   ♦

LAUGHING NOW

Something is happening to me
Something is bubbling in me
Like I'm about to laugh
Like I just heard the best news
Unexpected—yet a secret I've always known
I believe!
Like never before
I believe in Jesus
I believe what the Gospels tell
What the creeds confess
But it's more than that
How can I explain?
I believe in the greatest wonder of all
The Word became flesh!
So God could join us!
God becoming human to heal humanity
I believe Jesus is the all in all
All things summed up in him
I believe in the restoration of all things
Jesus is the Savior of the world!
It's more than the rescue of a few (lucky/elect) souls
Whisked off to heaven at the last second

As a consolation prize for a God whose plan didn't quite
       work out
Salvation belongs to the Lord
And it's bigger than we have imagined
I look at the Crucified and believe
I see perfect Love providing the Solution
Arms outstretched to embrace even enmity
Healing a world gone wrong with his wounds
Sin forgiven. Satan defeated. War abolished. Death
       destroyed. Creation restored.
I believe the mystic's thirteenth revelation of divine love
All shall be well, and all shall be well, and all manner of
       things shall be well
I didn't say I can explain it or defend it
But I believe it!
I believe the Gospel John gave
The Galilean prophet who is I AM
Bread. Light. Gate. Shepherd. Resurrection. Vine. Way.
       Truth. Life.
I believe we can eat his flesh and drink his blood
And live forever
I believe the vision John saw
New Jerusalem. New Heaven. New Earth.
I'm laughing now because I believe it when Jesus says—
Behold, I make all things new!
I'm laughing now because I believe that in the end
       love wins
Love believes all things and hopes all things
What would love believe about God? Believe that.
What would love hope for humanity? Hope that.
And laugh now
(If just for a little bit)

ACKNOWLEDGMENTS

Writing is lonely work, but writers are always tethered to friends and colleagues to whom they owe a debt of gratitude. Thanks to my agent, Andrea Heinecke, for her encouragement and ideas, and especially for her enthusiastic support. Thanks to Elissa Schauer and the many others at InterVarsity Press for their professionalism and editorial help in shaping this book into its final form. Thanks to the wonderful leadership team at Word of Life Church, without whom I could not pursue my dual vocation of pastor and author—I count them as both colleagues and friends.

Thanks to António Lobo Antunes for the inspiration, even though he doesn't believe in inspiration. (Why, Carlos?) Thanks to a triumvirate of towering intellects from a bygone era to whom so much of the thinking in this book is indebted: Friedrich Nietzsche, Søren Kierkegaard, and Fyodor Dostoevsky. (I hope in the age to come to meet all three.)

Someone once said that to be happy in life we only need three things: something to be passionate about, something to look forward to, and someone to share it with. I believe this is probably true. So I thank my friends. Jason Upton—the ideas set forth in this book were first conceived as we talked about "deconstruction" in a Belfast pub. Kenneth Tanner—who embodies what it means to be a wise pastor when everything is on fire. Joe Beach—our friendship began over a shared love of Bob Dylan sixteen years ago but has grown into a deep brotherhood. Brad Jersak—so much of the thinking in this book was honed in conversation with this keen theologian and dear friend. (Also, I must thank Brad for his very generous foreword.)

Since these are "acknowledgments," I want to acknowledge that in this book I am primarily writing for my grandchildren—Jude, Finn, Evey, Liam, Mercy, Hope, Pax, and Honor. This is part of my humble attempt to help make Christianity possible for them and their generation.

Finally, thanks to my first editor, soulmate, life companion, and best friend—Peri Zahnd. For the sake of variety I dedicate my books to different people, but every book I've ever written or ever will write is really dedicated to her.

NOTES

1 THE MADMAN'S LANTERN

[1]*The Lord of the Rings: The Fellowship of the Ring*, directed by Peter Jackson (Burbank, CA: New Line Cinema, 2001).

[2]Friedrich Nietzsche, *The Gay Science: With a Prelude in Rhymes and an Appendix of Songs*, trans. Walter Kaufman (New York: Vintage Books, 1974), 181.

[3]Nietzsche, *Gay Science*, 182.

[4]Nietzsche, *Gay Science*, 279.

[5]For Nietzsche, the overman would be male and male only since his view of women was quite low. He said, "Women are still cats, and birds. Or at best, cows." Friedrich Nietzsche, *Thus Spoke Zarathustra*, trans. Clancy Martin (New York: Barnes & Noble Classics, 2005), 26.

[6]Nietzsche, *Thus Spoke Zarathustra*, 13.

[7]Friedrich Nietzsche, *Twilight of the Idols* (Indianapolis: Hackett, 1997), 6.

[8]Jacques Derrida, quoted in Friedrich Nietzsche, *Why I Am So Wise*, trans. R. J. Hollingdale (London: Penguin, 2004), 59.

[9]Nietzsche, *Zarathustra*, 310.

[10]Nietzsche, *Gay Science*, 182.

[11]Kenneth Lantz, *The Dostoevsky Encyclopedia* (Westport, CT: Greenwood Press, 204), 21.

[12]Søren Kierkegaard, *Attack Upon "Christendom"* (Princeton, NJ: Princeton University Press, 1944), 126.

2 DECONSTRUCTING DECONSTRUCTION

[1]Randy S. Woodley, *Shalom and the Community of Creation* (Grand Rapids, MI: Eerdmans, 2012), 68.

[2]The remainder of this section is lightly adapted from Brian Zahnd, foreword to Austin Fisher, *Faith in the Shadows: Christ in the Midst of Doubt* (Downers Grove, IL: InterVarsity Press, 2018).

[3]The material in this and the following paragraph is adapted from a post by the author: Brian Zahnd, "Deconstruction or Restoration," Brian Zahnd (blog), April 27, 2016, https://brianzahnd.com/2016/04/deconstruction-or-restoration.

[4]John D. Caputo, *Deconstruction in a Nutshell: A Conversation with Jacques Derrida* (New York: Fordham University Press, 1997), 32.

[5]Cornel West, *The Cornel West Reader* (New York: Civitas Books, 2000), 132.

3 THE DAY DERRIDA DIED

[1]Fyodor Dostoevsky, *The Idiot*, trans. Richard Pevear and Larissa Volokhonsky (New York: Everyman's Library, 2002), 382.

[2]Ken Follett, *Notre-Dame: A Short History of the Meaning of Cathedrals* (New York: Viking, 2019), 9.

[3]Follett, *Notre-Dame*, 7.

[4]Joni Mitchell, *Big Yellow Taxi*, Reprise, 1970.

[5]Elian Peltier, et al., "Notre-Dame Came Far Closer to Collapsing Than People Knew," *New York Times*, July 18, 2019, www.nytimes.com/interactive/2019/07/16/world/europe/notre-dame.html.

[6]Victor Hugo, *The Hunchback of Notre Dame* (London: CRW Publishing Limited, 2004), bk. 7, chap. 1.

4 THE END IS THE BEGINNING

[1]Blaise Pascal, *Pensées* 423, trans. A. J. Krailsheimer (New York: Penguin, 1966), 154.

[2]Voltaire, "Letter to the Author of Three Imposters," 1770.

[3]Cynthia Bourgeault, *The Meaning of Mary Magdalene: Discovering the Woman at the Heart of Christianity* (Boulder, CO: Shambhala, 2010), 15.

[4]There are those who use the term *historical Jesus* to differentiate from the *Christ of faith*. But I refuse these differentiations. The historical Jesus is the Christ of faith—but it is only the Christ of faith that we have real access to.

[5]Ignatius IV, *The Resurrection and Modern Man* (Crestwood, NY: St. Vladimir's Seminary Press, 1985), 73.

[6]Stanley Hauerwas introduced me to this concept: "Evangelicals have two things: Jesus and energy. And I admire both!" I agree with this insight—evangelicals *do* have energy. Stanley Hauerwas, "Stanley Hauerwas on His Evangelical Audience," YouTube, accessed February 25, 2021, www.youtube.com/watch?v=jGsay7xmB7s.

[7]T. S. Eliot, "Four Quartets," *Collected Poems 1909-1962* (Orlando: Harcourt, 1968), 208.

5 LOSING JESUS

[1]Leszek Kolakowski, quoted in Gerhard Lohfink, *No Irrelevant Jesus*, trans. Linda M. Maloney (Collegeville, MN: Liturgical Press, 2014), 2.

[2]Fyodor Dostoevsky, *The Brothers Karamazov*, trans. Richard Pevear and Larissa Volokhonsky (San Francisco: North Point Press, 1990), 249.

[3]Dostoevsky, *Brothers Karamazov*, 249-50.

[4]Dostoevsky, *Brothers Karamazov*, 250.

[5]Dostoevsky, *Brothers Karamazov*, 252.

[6]Dostoevsky, *Brothers Karamazov*, 258.

[7]Dostoevsky, *Brothers Karamazov*, 260.

[8]Dostoevsky, *Brothers Karamazov*, 262.

[9]Dostoevsky, *Brothers Karamazov*, 259.

[10]Dostoevsky, *Brothers Karamazov*, 263.

[11]Dostoevsky, *Brothers Karamazov*, 322.

[12]M. Craig Barnes, *When God Interrupts: Finding New Life Through Unwanted Change* (Downers Grove, IL: InterVarsity Press, 1996), 123.

6 THE DARK NIGHT OF UNKNOWING

[1]George MacDonald, *Lilith* (Doylestown, PA: Wildside Press, 2002), 20.

[2]Bruce Cockburn, "Pacing the Cage," *Jan Douwe Kroeske Presents: 2 Meter Sessions #712*, 2020.

[3]Aleksandr Solzhenitsyn, *The Gulag Archipelago*, pt. 4, *The Soul and Barbed Wire* (New York: HarperCollins, 1974), 613.

[4]N. T. Wright, *Paul: A Biography* (New York: HarperCollins, 2018), 52.

7 THE ONLY FOUNDATION

[1]Karl Barth, *Church Dogmatics*, vol. 1: *The Doctrine of the Word of God*, pt. 2 (Peabody, MA: Hendrickson, 1956), 21.

[2]Douglas A. Campbell, *Pauline Dogmatics* (Grand Rapids, MI: Eerdmans, 2020), 40-41.

[3]William Shakespeare, *Hamlet*, act 1, scene 5.

[4]Ken Ham is a young earth creationist and the founder and CEO of Answers in Genesis, the organization that operates the Creation Museum and Ark Experience in Kentucky.

[5]See Saint Anselm of Canterbury, *Proslogion*, written in 1077–1078, available here: https://web.archive.org/web/19970512040225/http://www3.baylor.edu/~Scott_Moore/Anselm/Proslogion.html.

[6]James H. Cone, "Christianity and Black Power," *Risks of Faith: The Emergence of a Black Theology of Liberation, 1968–1998* (Boston: Beacon, 1999), 14-15.

8 ALL ALONE UPSTAIRS

[1]René Descartes, quoted in A. C. Grayling, *Descartes: The Life and Times of a Genius* (New York: Walker, 2005), 162-63.

[2]Elizabeth A. Johnson, *Ask the Beasts: Darwin and the God of Love* (London: Bloomsbury, 2014), 126.

[3]Ludwig Wittgenstein, *Tractatus Logico-Philosophicus* (New York: Dover, 1998), 89.

[4]Søren Kierkegaard, *Concluding Unscientific Postscript to Philosophical Fragments*, ed. and trans. Howard V. Hong (Princeton, NJ: Princeton University Press, 1992), 1:335.

[5]Blaise Pascal, *Pensées*, trans. A. J. Krailsheimer (London: Penguin, 1966), 285-86.

[6]Pascal, *Pensées*, 127.

[7]Søren Kierkegaard, *Provocations: Spiritual Writings of Kierkegaard*, comp. and ed. Charles E. Moore (Maryknoll, NY: Orbis, 2003), 78-79.

[8]Moore, *Provocations*, xxvi.

[9]There is a left-wing postmodernity that many of us contend leads only to nihilism. But there is a right-wing postmodernity that moves past modernity's dead end of critiquing all traditions by finding a framing story in some older tradition. For me that older tradition is Christianity, but that tradition must be lived. It's what Kierkegaard meant when he said, "All truth inheres in subjectivity."

[10]Sergius Bulgakov, *Unfading Light*, trans. Thomas Allan Smith (Grand Rapids, MI: Eerdmans, 2012), 10.

9 A MYSTIC OR NOTHING AT ALL

[1]Karl Rahner, *Opportunities for Faith: Elements of a Modern Spirituality*, trans. Edward Quinn (New York: Seabury, 1974), 123.

[2]Karl Rahner, *The Mystical Way in Everyday Life*, trans. Annemarie S. Kidder (Maryknoll, NY: Orbis, 2010), xxi.
[3]Kidder, *Mystical Way*, xvii.
[4]I tell this story in the beginning of my book *A Farewell to Mars* (Colorado Springs, CO: David C. Cook, 2014).

10 THE GRACE OF SECOND NAIVETÉ

[1]Walter Brueggemann, *Praying the Psalms: Engaging Scripture and the Life of the Spirit*, 2nd ed. (Eugene, OR: Cascade Books, 2007), 3.
[2]David Bentley Hart, *The New Testament: A Translation* (New Haven, CT: Yale University Press, 2019), 336.
[3]Gerhard Lohfink, *No Irrelevant Jesus*, trans. Linda M. Maloney (Collegeville, MN: Liturgical Press, 2014), 314.
[4]C. S. Lewis, dedication to *The Lion, the Witch and the Wardrobe*, Chronicles of Narnia (New York: HarperTrophy, 1994).
[5]Walt Whitman, "Passage to India," in *Leaves of Grass* (New York: Barnes & Noble Books, 1993), 345.
[6]Gustavo Gutiérrez, *On Job: God-Talk and the Suffering of the Innocent* (Maryknoll, NY, Orbis Books, 1987), 1.
[7]William Shakespeare, *Hamlet*, act 3, scene 1.
[8]Lewis, *Lion, the Witch and the Wardrobe*, 188.

11 THE HOUSE OF LOVE

[1]Henri J. M. Nouwen, *Behold the Beauty of the Lord: Praying with Icons* (Notre Dame, IN: Ave Maria Press, 1987), 30-31.
[2]See Jared Diamond, *Germs, Guns, and Steel: The Fates of Human Societies* (New York: Norton, 1999).
[3]Karl Rahner, *Karl Rahner in Dialogue: Conversations and Interviews 1965-1982* (Spring Valley, NY: Crossroad, 1986), 207.
[4]Julian of Norwich, *Revelations of Divine Love*, ed. Halcyon Backhouse (London: Hodder & Stoughton, 1987), 86.
[5]Lazar Puhalo, personal correspondence with author, May 27, 2019.
[6]David Bentley Hart, *Theological Territories* (Notre Dame, IN: Notre Dame Press, 2020), 115.

CONCLUSION: EVERY BUSH ABLAZE

[1]Elizabeth Barrett Browning, *Aurora Leigh* (Oxford: Oxford University Press, 2008), 245.